Praise for Big as the Whole Wide World

Sherle Stevens is an exquisite writer whose life story captivates like an adventure novel. Filled with pain, joy, heartbreak, and redemption, her journey reveals the sacredness of every relationship and how even the most challenging can be a doorway to your own ultimate peace and freedom.

- Debra Poneman, bestselling author and founder of Yes To Success and Ageless seminars.

I love this book. Clear-eyed, forgiving and filled with adventure, Sherle's story is both deeply personal and universal. Somehow, through her words, I found myself reflecting more kindly on my own missteps and belly-flops - and even feeling more generous toward those who have wounded me. This story is a living testament to the adage that "everyone is always doing the best they can with the information they have at the time, and when you know better, you do better."

- Sam Bennett, bestselling author of *Get It Done, Start Right Where You Are*, and *The 15-Minute Method*.

Reading Big As The Whole Wide World will feel like a gift to you if you struggle with the relationship you have with your mother or adult daughter. Sherle Stevens' memoir helped me understand my mother in a way that she hasn't or won't be able

to show me. Let this brilliant book be a balm to the painful unanswered questions that haunt you.
- Karen C.L. Anderson, master-certified life coach and bestselling author of several books including: *You Are Not Your Mother: Releasing Generational Trauma and Shame,* and *Difficult Mothers, Adult Daughters: A Guide for Separation, Liberation, and Inspiration.* She is also the host of the Dear Adult Daughter Podcast and founder of Shame School.

PRAISE FOR SHERLE STEVEN'S WORKBOOK: THE NUMEROLOGY PLAYBOOK

Finally, a practical, step-by-step guide to unlocking the secrets of numerology. Stevens provides just enough information so that learning about your gifts, challenges and best way forward can be a revelation rather than a confusing task. I can personally attest to the author's experience and skill as both a gifted practitioner and teacher. The design and format of the Playbook support the learning in every way.
- Katie Carlone, Master Coach and Life Strategist

Excellent overview of numerology and how to work your own numbers. Workbook format with easy to understand instructions. Highly recommend for those interested in keeping track of their own numbers and applying to their lives.
- Kristin S. Kaufman, Leadership Coach

While this is an enjoyable read, it's extremely informative as

well. The author offers a guided pathway to understanding oneself, which is an invaluable tool.
- Carolyn B., Amazon Reviewer

Sherle Stevens, you are the best! Thank you for contributing such a valuable, entertaining book. This world needs more knowledge and love which this book is very good source. You inspire folks like me to continue to open the eyes of our fellow human beings through numbers. Again, thank you.
-Marilee Arvin, Numerologist

I love this book! This book is filled with much knowledge and wisdom but broken down in a very simplistic way that is easy to understand and instantly start using. Sherle is a truly master of symbolic systems, and truly gifted teacher. I have grown so much working with the content in this book and I love how practical it is and how simply it is organized. If you are interested in Numerology, this book will be a tremendous help in your learning process. And if you are already versed in numerology, this book will increase your understanding & knowledge. I would highly recommend this book to anyone learning or expanding their knowledge of numerology.
-Stacy H. Quast, Intuitive Astrology

BIG AS THE WHOLE WIDE WORLD
FINDING PEACE BEYOND MY KARMIC FAMILY TIES

SHERLE STEVENS

ML STIMPSON ENTERPRISES

Copyright © 2024 by Sherle Stevens

Published by M L Stimpson Enterprises

P.O. Box 1592

Cedar Hill, TX 75106-1592

Print ISBN: 978-1-943563-38-8

Hardcover ISBN: 978-1-943563-39-5

Ebook ISBN: 978-1-943563-37-1

All rights reserved.

No part of this book may be reproduced in any form or by any electronic or mechanical means, including information storage and retrieval systems, without written permission from the author, except for the use of brief quotations in a book review.

This memoir is a recollection of events as experienced and remembered by the author. While every effort has been made to ensure the accuracy of the details, most names have been changed to respect the privacy of individuals.

Dedication

*For Grace,
For all Time*

*But little by little,
as you left their voices behind,
the stars began to burn
through the sheets of clouds,
and there was a new voice
which you slowly
recognized as your own,
that kept you company
as you strode deeper and deeper
into the world,
determined to do
the only thing you could do—
determined to save
the only life you could save.*

*— Mary Oliver
from* The Journey

Contents

Preface · xv
Author's Note · xvii

Book One: Debut

Prelude · 3

Chapter 1 · 7
STARTING OUT: Deciding Whether to Stay or Go 1940

Chapter 2 · 14
GETTING OUT: Movies and Dreams 1940-1955

Chapter 3 · 30
SPREADING OUT: Out of High School and Off to College 1956-1959

Book Two: Performance

Chapter 4 · 37
DROPPING OUT: Meeting Jack, Leaving School, Living In Sin 1959-1961

Chapter 5 · 51
WAITING IT OUT: Working Two Jobs 1961

Chapter 6 · 59
STEPPING OUT: Into the World, at last 1962

Chapter 7 · 65
TURNING OUT: Holland/England 1962

Chapter 8 · 75
FINDING OUT: England, Married, Pregnant, Blind 1962

Chapter 9 · 86
LOOKING OUT: For myself and my baby 1962

Chapter 10 · 92
LUCKING OUT: A New and Happy Life 1963-1965

Chapter 11   100
TRYING OUT: New York! Testing my talent 1965

Chapter 12   105
STILL TRYING: Paul, School, First Day at McCalls 1965

Chapter 13   116
FREAKING OUT: Blackout - November 9, 1965

Chapter 14   121
LEAVING OUT: A Big Detail, Blizzard, Taxi, Gone 1965

Chapter 15   125
COMING OUT #1: Christopher, Ted 1965

Chapter 16   133
SNEAKING OUT: Falling For Ted 1965

Chapter 17   140
MOVING OUT - Divorce/ Betrayal 1973

Chapter 18   147
CRYING OUT: Leaving Ted, Salt Lake City 1973 -1975

Chapter 19   156
SEARCHING OUT: Salt Lake City, Las Vegas 1975 - 77

Chapter 20   167
SPINNING OUT: Of control, Jenny in Dallas 1977-1996

Chapter 21   181
MAKING OUT/ FALLING OUT: Freelance / Brad / Bankrupt 1982-85

Chapter 22   190
REACHING OUT: Travel Agent 1997

BOOK THREE: ENCORE

Chapter 23   197
COMING OUT #2: Falling For Grace -1997

Chapter 24   206
LEAPING OUT: Into Italy 1997

Chapter 25   212
WORKING IT OUT: Visiting Jenny 1999 – 2015

Chapter 26   223
STANDING OUT: New York, Daring to Sing 2003

Chapter 27   229
LOSING OUT: Gone 2003-2005

Chapter 28   234
TIME OUT: The Camino de Santiago 2012

Chapter 29   247
MORE TIME OUT: Pilgrimage 2013

BOOK FOUR: COMEBACK

Chapter 30   269
FIGURING IT OUT: Breakthrough! 2022

Chapter 31   274
BIG AS THE WHOLE WIDE WORLD: Michael – 2021

Chapter 32   281
HELPING OUT: May others find their healing – 2023

Chapter 33   289
January 2023

Epilogue   291

Afterword   305

About the Author   309

Acknowledgments   311

Resources   315

Preface

Karma is a concept of Hinduism which describes a system in which beneficial effects are derived from past beneficial actions and harmful effects from past harmful actions, creating a system of actions and reactions throughout a soul's reincarnated lives, forming a cycle of rebirth.

In each incarnation, we bring in past-life relationships in order to heal our karma. We have a lot of unfinished business.

It's possible to heal our karma with a person, even if they don't heal their karma with us in this lifetime. In that case, they will have to work it out with someone else who has an energy similar to ours.

In my story, you will discover my karmic relationships, most of whom were family ties, beginning with the family I was born into. Three of them I married, one I loved and lost, and one I gave birth to.

Author's Note

I feel like I have been waiting for something all my life. Waiting to be held, to be touched, to be loved. Waiting in the fall for school to begin, waiting for my birthday, waiting for spring. I waited to become special, to be chosen. Mostly, I was impatiently waiting to grow up and get out and find the world. And when that time came, I didn't wait any longer. I got up and left and tried to find what I wanted. To make it happen for me. Sometimes that worked, often it didn't.

This is not the book I thought I would write. At first, I intended only to leave my younger friends a small book with the details of my adventures, my passions, my travels...but the lessons and the healings are important. I kept writing, and so much more poured out. Through the good times and the awful, feeling ecstatic and sometimes devastated, I've lived to learn what it took to find my way home to myself.

You'll see how many mistakes I continued to make because for so long there was a lot about life that I failed to understand. Eventually, I began to forgive myself for those mistakes.

All of that is in here, but what I feel may be most important to share with you is the story of how I lost my loving relationship with my daughter Jenny, and later found peace. Through embracing the loving friendship of others, I found that under that pain, peace and even joy had been here all along. To realize that, I had only to let go of what I could not change. Of what was not mine to hold on to.

I had thrown away all the journals that reminded me of the anguish I'd felt during so much of our past five decades together – pain she always seemed to be feeling too. So, I've had to rely on memory in reconstructing our dynamic.

In the beginning I was afraid that writing about this time with her could take away some of the serenity that has come to me over the past six years. I was concerned too that it could upset my partner Grace for me to be living this heartbreaking relationship all over again, asking her questions to help me remember what she had seen and heard that I could not be sure of.

Then I remembered this powerful instruction from the spiritual teacher and author Andrew Harvey. He has said that whatever breaks your heart the most - that's where your passion is, where your mission lies. That's what has given me the courage to put all of this into words, hoping that it will help others find peace and healing too.

If this is your story, my arms are around you. May you be able to find peace as I have, as Grace and I have, and as I hope Jenny will find in her own time.

Book One: Debut

Prelude

This time I had to trust the Universe. There was nothing else left to trust – not even my own knowing. Especially not that.

I grabbed my backpack and got off the train from Paris, looking down at my boots barely in time to notice my first step on this 500-mile trek – the pilgrimage that is the Camino de Santiago de Compostela in Spain.

I didn't know why I had come, only that I had felt a calling a year earlier, and it came with an urgency that both excited and calmed me to trust it. Not having any other solution left, I began a months-long training for this extraordinary hike, and now I had arrived.

As you might imagine, things were not well in my world, and I was grateful to have the calling to hang onto.

In fact, things were a mess. The relationship I was in was disintegrating. I had no idea what I was going to do with my life when I returned. Not to put too fine a point on it – but I would soon be turning 75. Pretty late in the game to be looking for answers.

Wasn't I supposed to have things figured out by now?

But then I'd always been asking these questions of Life. Who am I? Why am I here? And why have I always felt different somehow? Not quite comfortable in my own skin.

I grew up in the Midwest. Pleasant in the summer; glorious in autumn; drab in the winter; promising in the spring. In the 1950s very conservative. Not a natural habitat for a child who dreamed of far-off adventure, of magic, and of big and exciting dreams coming true. This was a part of the country that the people I would soon long to meet were flying over, rushing back to their exciting lives in New York City and Los Angeles.

If anyone was looking in the window at us, everything must have seemed normal. My daddy went to work and came home every evening. He was gentle and kind. I knew he loved me. He called me his Dollbaby. He brought me my favorite comic books if ever I was sick in bed, and never said a harsh word to me in all his life.

Daddy always had a little smile, though he didn't say much in the evenings after supper. It didn't matter; I was just content to be sitting on the floor in the living room, coloring pictures. He listened to anything I wanted to tell him, and he was very proud of my little drawings.

Mother was beautiful, with a particularly engaging smile, and seemed gracious to everyone. She kept a clean and lovely home, running the household, cooking delicious meals, making not only my childhood dresses on her sewing-machine, but the living-room drapes and slipcovers as well. She made sure I was given regular visits to the dentist and private lessons in drawing, tap-dancing, acting, and swimming in the summer. She always attended the parent-teacher meetings at my schools and supervised my homework.

Meeting the parents of my school friends, I always felt like I had the best ones. I thought of my parents as happily married because they seemed content with each other and there was never any quarreling. They were all I had – there were no sisters or brothers to play with, or to talk to. Daddy was gone all day long and Mother was busy. So, after school I just played quietly by myself with my paper dolls, and colored pictures with my crayons, and read my storybooks. To that someone looking in the window, it would surely have seemed that this was all I needed.

If that had been the whole story, I might have led a different life, and would never have written this book.

But why don't I begin at the beginning?

ONE
STARTING OUT: DECIDING WHETHER TO STAY OR GO 1940

I lay on my back in my crib late one summer evening looking up at the ceiling... wondering...should I go or should I stay?

I was seldom touched by the cold and remote woman who was always in another room, away from me. She was my mother. My heart hurt. I didn't think I could handle the weight of staying here, of having a life, if she was in charge of it. It seemed like too heavy a load. I felt it would mean that my heart would always be hurting.

It was late evening, and the objects in my room were already in silhouette against the darkening night sky. I thought I could see a Chinese man sitting in a chair at the end of the room looking back at me.

Somehow, I knew if I went back to where I had come from (what I would many years later refer to as God or Divine

Source) I would be given a chance of finding new parents. I wanted a Mommy who would cuddle me, spend time with me, and make me feel loved and wanted and safe. Of course, as I was weighing the options, it only made sense that I would have to start over as a tiny helpless baby. I knew I was older than that now, feeling stronger. I could walk, so now I was seldom held. Yes, I felt alone. But still... sometimes my mother would break off little squares of a Hershey bar and give me tiny bites.

And I reasoned that I was getting this treat because I was older, that tiny babies don't get chocolate. So, I stayed.

I've always felt that having this memory is a remarkable gift. It's how I know that I was conscious and alert to my mother and my feelings about her, and about my life from nearly the beginning.

I remember telling part of the story to my girlfriends in high school in a self-deprecating way, adding that it must be why I had always loved sweets, and was never quite as slender as they were. Nobody remarked that it was unusual to remember being a baby, especially one who had ideas already, and who made decisions. Of course, I left out the part of feeling sad about my mother.

Not until after my father died when I was 32 did I learn my mother's family secret. Her sister Neva Grace had died on the operating table from an ectopic pregnancy while my mother was carrying me.

Did my mother decide then that she didn't want me? Was it unseemly for her to be delivering a healthy baby after her sister died in the attempt - a tragedy that sent my grandmother into a mental spiral from which she never fully recovered?

I don't know. Maybe my mother didn't want a child in the first place. But she did work hard with what was dealt to her. My daddy earned a living, but she managed the bills and the household. I was just her "responsibility" as she pointed out to me more than 50 years later when I asked her what I was like as a little girl. I was then deep in the throes of therapy and curious about how I had seemed to her then. When she paused, I offered suggestions. Was I shy and quiet? Or bouncy and happy-go-lucky? It seemed beyond her to recall. But I didn't need to ask; I was certain that when I was very young, I'd been quiet, not wanting to disturb.

Probably the best part of what she accomplished was seeing to it that I had the benefit of braces on my teeth, and a good education embellished with those private lessons, especially the drawing classes, which paid off well in my long career as a working artist.

Since I was her job and she was serious about doing it well, she was very critical. She expected me to excel in all my classes; even a B on a report card was unacceptable. I watched her facial expressions to gauge her mood so I could stay out of her way as much as possible.

Sometimes she would tear off green branches from the bushes in the yard and whip my legs. She called this switching, and it made stinging welts on my legs. Worse, it was a punishment – but for what?

"Please don't hit me! I'll be good!" I screamed every time. Maybe I had asked too many questions. Or voiced my feelings about something she'd said.

"Don't dispute me!" I heard often. But I didn't know why I wasn't allowed to say what I felt. She did. I was always frightened of her, even as I longed for her love. The fear remained even when I finally became a grownup myself.

Whenever we visited my mother's sisters, my Aunt Thelma and Aunt Eileen, they would gather in another room, away from me. I could hear my mother talking to them and laughing in tones that didn't even sound like her voice. When she was with them, she had little interest in me. It was like they were a closed group, and I was not invited in. I began to think of them as the Pretty Girls Club.

I must have looked sad a lot when she returned to the room where I was sitting, because she would admonish me. "Stop pouting!" and "Quit feeling sorry for yourself!" And I would be thinking, *there's a lot to feel sorry about here*. But I said nothing. Often my stomach hurt, and the insides of my mouth would have canker sores, which she would medicate with powdered alum.

When I was nearly five years old, my mother took me to visit Aunt Eileen and her little girl, who was not quite three. Carol Jean was adorable. Aunt Eileen's eyes were bright with happiness, watching her tiny daughter, and cooing to her. "Oh, my little chickadee! You are my sweet little pookie!," she said. I was fascinated at these terms of endearment. Later I asked my mother why she didn't call me special names like that. "I think it's silly," she said, with disdain. I decided I wasn't adorable enough for dear little names like those.

Yet there were times of sweetness. Often, evenings after dinner we would have dishes of ice cream or have popcorn and soda-pop, just for the two of us. Daddy didn't like such treats. And in the afternoons, she would sometimes lie down on the couch, and hold out her arms to me.

"Come, give me a love," she would ask. I always hoped that instead she would say, "Come, let me love you." But that never happened. Still, it was a moment of relief from her critical comments.

I wanted so much to love her. My first time at sleep-away camp, I was in my bunk in the cabin when a rainy afternoon sent us indoors. My mother had sent me a postcard in the mail, telling me she hoped I was having a good time. Just seeing her pretty handwriting made my eyes water and my nose burn. It was such an unexpectedly loving message, and I felt guilty that I had had so many bad thoughts about her. I wanted to believe then that she really did love me.

Many years later as she lay dying in her 80s, I stood in the doorway of her hospital room, watching the nurses surrounding her. When they told me she had taken her last breath, I felt a sudden exhale and realized that I finally felt safe. I was free.

An hour later in a restaurant with my aunt and uncle I fell

apart, shuddering with relief from the fear I'd carried silently all my life. I was nearly 54.

The fact that I had no siblings though all my friends did, made me feel that my mother didn't want any more children, and that must be because I was somehow a disappointment, or a burden.

But maybe it was just that she already had enough work managing me.

There were no other family members around since all my parents' relatives lived in another state. They refused to tell me about their lives before I was born, though I longed to know who they were, and where I came from. The total information my mother offered: my parents met in a drugstore in Michigan. They won Charleston contests in the early 1930s. That was it. Until one day a big secret came out.

On a childhood trip to that state, my parents dropped me off for the day at the home of one of my father's sisters. It turned out to be at the same time her grandchildren, a teen-age brother and sister who lived in Chicago, introduced to me as my cousins, were also visiting. When the grownups weren't around, they taunted me.

"Your father was married before to somebody else!" What? I'd not yet heard of divorce in the 1950's. "And she ran away!" they continued.

Oh no. I couldn't imagine that anyone would leave my sweet Daddy. But - wait a minute! Maybe that woman could be my real mother. And that would explain why the woman who was posing as my mother was so cold and critical of me. I was elated. Overjoyed to think that was why this "mother" treated me like she did. I didn't belong to her.

I ran off the porch and into the house to ask a grownup if it was true. *Yes!* My aunt told me that his first wife's name was Dorothy. I knew that Dorothy was written as the Mother's name on my Birth Certificate. My Daddy had married two women named Dorothy.

I held my breath, praying that the first Dorothy was my real mother. And that would mean that the one I was afraid of must be my stepmother. I'd read enough fairy tales when I was younger to know they are always mean, and the *real* Mommies are always kind and loving. Maybe my real Mommy was out there somewhere now, missing me and trying to find me.

But then my aunt added the part that burst my hopes; that had all happened nine years before I was born. Here I was only 13 - so for her to have been my real mother, I would now have to be 22. Oh, please *no!* Just when everything was beginning to make sense to me.

And the woman who evidently was my real mother *was* mean; although she no longer switched me, her criticism was mean enough. I was sad for my Daddy too, that he had been hurt and left behind.

He lived another twenty years, and I never told him what I knew. It would be another *fifty* years before I would even begin to understand all of this.

Two
GETTING OUT: MOVIES AND DREAMS
1940-1955

After that night when I decided to stay, I began trying to memorize the events of my little life, figuring that eventually I would be old enough to understand myself; to know why I felt sad, or scared, when I did. And who was I, anyway? I hoped to have someone explain it all to me.

When I was 5, something glorious and magical arrived in my life and changed it forever, the wonderful world of the movies. Not the cartoons. I was through with them when I was 3 when the unbearable happened, and Bambi's mother was killed. She had been a kind mother and suddenly was gone, and Bambi was alone. I couldn't bear the pain I felt at the thought of losing a Mommy like that.

No. I mean the real movies that showed me that there were other, different kinds of people in the world. I desperately wanted to get out there and find them. I wanted the hugs and the laughter they so easily shared with one another.

Most of all, I was in bliss watching the marvelous dancing and listening to the beautiful songs in all those M-G-M musicals. I was dazzled by the flash and brilliance of the spotlights on their faces, all the tapping feet, all the glamour and the lights and the magic.

By the time I was a teenager it was the glorious stories in the movies that I loved the most- the tales of The Girl who would go to New York and find The Boy. Oh, the wonderful singing and dancing as they created their exciting lives together, bubbling with joy and romance, finding thrilling success!

The daring, the adventure, the stars in their eyes, the happy endings! I was swept up in it at every Saturday matinee, and it lived in my daydreams all week long.

On the radio in the kitchen, I memorized all the songs on *Your Hit Parade*, singing along with Judy Garland and Frank Sinatra, Bing Crosby and Nat King Cole. I still remember singing the song "Nature Boy" on my way home from school one day, walking past the pretty hollyhocks edging the alley. That haunting melody was so emotional to me even then, at 8 years old. I love it still. And the lyrics...so different from all the love songs. They were the reflections of a seeker, like me.

As I was growing up, I always knew I would leave home after college and I would get to New York myself! Of course, I had no idea what I would do once I got there. But I knew it was in the cards, for sure.

When I was quite young, I had the thought that I was like a well, but the bucket that held the secrets that would explain everything to me was down so deep that I couldn't pull it up by myself. I hoped that when I was older, someone else, a grownup, would be able to pull it up and then I would understand who I was, what had been happening to me, and why. Mostly I needed to know why my mother was so cold and distant, and why she frightened me.

The biggest question for me - when I was trying to understand our mortality was to ask my mother "Why we are here?" And she said, "We're here to help *others*." Her voice sounded pinched and joyless, as if this were a heavy responsibility. There was no note that I could hear in her voice of wanting to help others from feeling compassion for them. I immediately felt excluded from the "others" so I turned to trying to find meaning for myself. Years later it occurred to me how different it would have felt to me to have heard a joyous, "We're here to *help each other*!" Then I would have felt included. And I might have learned a lot earlier how to do that, how to be helpful.

When it was time to buy new clothes for school, my mother and I would ride the bus downtown to go shopping. We had a car, but of course my father drove that to work. One day on the bus, before we were near the nice part of downtown where all the "good" department stores were, I looked out the window and saw only dark, dirty old buildings that I'd never noticed before. There were a few people walking about. They looked dirty and seemed old too. And they were hurting; I could feel it. This was the first time I'd seen poor people and my eyes filled with tears. How could this be happening? Why weren't people helping them?

"Ohh, Mommy, Look! Those poor people!!" I said.

My mother glanced out the window and sniffed as she turned away, saying, "They could at least afford soap!"

How could she say this when she'd told me that we were here to help people?

"Mommy, I don't think they even have enough to eat!" I cried. My heart hurt for them and for myself, with a mother who seemed not to care at all about something that felt tragic to me.

It was my second-grade teacher who taught me kindness. All I see in my mind's eye is an extreme closeup of Mrs. Figel's face, leaning over and smiling gently at me. I can only see her eyes and her smile. I can't really remember what the rest of her looked like at all. I have a vague sense of dark grey hair, maybe pulled back and pinned up. I was simply embraced by the way her eyes and her smile felt to my heart, which filled to overflowing with gratitude for her kindness to me. That this brief instant, recalled so often in my life, can always bring tears to my eyes makes me believe that Mrs. Figel awakened in me at that moment, the kindness in my own heart.

I've been forever thankful that from then on, kindness became the most important virtue to me; what I wanted most to feel within myself, and for others. It's the soul quality that I have always looked for and responded to in making new friends. Pity I didn't look for it when I fell in love.

Watching my mother around her friends, my father's friends, my teachers, the dentist or the doctor, she was interested and vivacious. Her expression looked so warm, so attentive, as if she were just delighted to see that person. Alone at home with me, she was not like that. When the door closed, her face changed. Serious now, no longer relaxed and happy.

So enthralled with the beautiful women I watched in the movies, I once asked her if I would be beautiful when I grew up.

"You'll be attractive," she said. "Attractive" is the loveliest I've ever managed to feel.

We moved to a house out in the countryside when I was in the third grade. There weren't regular streets like I had always known, just a big two-lane highway right at the edge of the small area of grass in front of the house. And houses were mostly miles apart. But there was a woman who lived across the driveway from us. She had three soft little kittens she let me hold in my lap, sitting on her back step. She said I could have one, and I begged for it, but my mother wouldn't hear of it.

Then one Sunday afternoon shortly after that, we were visiting Mother's friend, Louise, who lived not very far down the highway from us. Louise showed us a little Collie puppy, the only one left from a small litter. Mother asked me if I wanted her, and I was so excited that she would let me have a pet. When we got home, I couldn't wait to hold the squirmy little thing, hoping she would calm down so I could pet her, like the kittens. But my mother would not allow her to come into the house, so little Curly had to live in a low makeshift enclosure Mother fixed up in the garage, just propping up two long pieces of wood in a corner. It didn't look tall enough or sturdy enough to me.

The next day we returned to Louise's home for a picnic in the afternoon. I pleaded with my mother to let my puppy stay in the house, just while we were gone.

"Absolutely not! I won't have an animal in the house! Ever!"

She was angry at the very idea. My father said nothing. Why did she let me have a pet if we couldn't make sure it was safe? I was so afraid that my little puppy would run out onto the highway and be hit by a car.

When we finally got home it was dark, and she was gone.

I screamed and Mother sent me to bed. I cried myself to

sleep. The next morning, she told me to go look for the dog on the highway before the school bus came. How could she want me to be walking on a busy highway with all those cars, trying to find my puppy, now almost surely run over and lying there all bloody? I felt sick.

My father jumped into this scene and told me,

"Don't worry, Dollbaby, I'll go find her!"

"Oh no, El! You'll be late for work", my mother protested.

But for the first and last time in memory – my father's decision was final. When he came home that night, he told me gently that he had found her. She had died but was not bloody. He said she just looked like she was sleeping. Someone had moved her off to the side of the road. He told me he had taken her to be buried. I was so grateful for his tenderness.

I viewed my mother through the dark lens of that day for a long, long time.

The Christmas I turned 9, Mother gave me a beautiful jewelry box that opened to reveal a dancing ballerina doll that began to turn around while music played. Beneath her were several little compartments lined in burgundy velvet. Mother had such refined taste, and this gift was so extraordinary. I felt like she must really love me to give me something so elegant.

A few days later her sister, my Aunt Thelma, who had no children, came to visit from Michigan, bringing Christmas presents for all of us. Her gift to me was a lovely jewelry box that also featured a dancing ballerina. But this one was not nearly so nice nor so precious to me, as the one my mother had given me. I thanked my aunt, telling her how much I loved it, and never mentioned the gift from my mother.

A few days later, Aunt Thelma returned to Michigan. I knew we wouldn't see her and my Uncle Don again until we went to their cottage at a small lake the following summer, as usual. Nevertheless, once she was gone, and over my protests, my mother took back her gift, saying she needed to return it to the store so her sister's feelings wouldn't be hurt. I put Aunt Thelma's gift on the floor of my closet, pushing it way to the back. My mother didn't seem to notice. Neither of us mentioned it again.

I never knew what happened that led to my mother spending six months in bed the following year, because no one would tell me. She wasn't ill. I do remember hearing the words "nervous breakdown" whispered, but I didn't know what that could mean. I was supposed to be quiet and not disturb her. Only my father could go into the bedroom. At some point Aunt Thelma returned.

One morning she asked me if I liked pancakes, and I said yes, I did. Soon she came to the table with a stack of them on the plate she set in front of me.

"I can only eat one pancake," I said.

"Well," she answered, "you said "yes" when I asked you so

now you have to eat all of them. You can't leave the table until you finish."

Why wasn't she eating some? Where was my Daddy? Didn't he need to eat some too? I couldn't understand why this was a meal fixed just for me. I ate the first one, not so delicious now with all the others waiting. I tried to keep chewing and just focus on Judy Garland on the kitchen radio. She was singing "Zing Went The Strings Of My Heart". I kept trying to swallow more pancake but suddenly *zing* went all those extra bites right back onto my plate. I left the table and ran to the bathroom. I couldn't look at a pancake again for another twenty years.

Looking back, it seems that my mother and Aunt Thelma must have been suffering from severe depression, or maybe even some other mental disorder. Families didn't talk about such things back then, and my family certainly never told me anything. Not even about my grandmother's unusual presence in a room, muttering softly under her breath, not making sense.

All I know is that by the time I was 11 years old, I wanted to die. I tried to smother myself with my pillow, but I couldn't seem to do it right. I was so upset at being such a coward that I wrote myself a note and saved it in a tin box of cough drops with a lid I'd painted over with rosy nail polish. I made a promise that if things weren't better by the time I was 12, I would figure out another more surefire way. I didn't even know what I was expecting to be better, except that it was about my mother, and my not hurting like this.

I always remembered my promise, but by the time I turned 12, I did feel better, and I decided that I wouldn't try to end my life again. I was getting closer to being old enough to go to college and I knew I could find a happier life somehow, out in the world, away from my mother. I began to feel hopeful, even excited.

One afternoon when I was 13, my 8th grade boyfriend walked me home from school. My mother had gone shopping, and she had told me never to let a boy in when she was not at home. But Kent wanted to see our new apartment, so I let him into the living room. He was a nice boy and didn't even try to kiss me before he left after a minute or two. We hadn't even sat down.

Nevertheless, I felt guilty, so when she returned, I told my mother I had broken the rule. I insisted that it was all perfectly innocent, and that I would never do it again. I just couldn't imagine doing something behind her back. I thought she would appreciate my honesty and my promise to behave as she'd instructed.

But without a word, she picked up the yardstick that she was now using to smack my legs, evidently too embarrassed to go out into the public yard where other people who lived in the apartment building would be able to see her tearing branches from a bush.

"I hope that when you grow up, you have a daughter who breaks your heart the way you've broken mine!" she snarled. It felt like a curse.

I had no idea how this could have broken her heart. But before she could hit me, I grabbed the yardstick from her hand, snapped it in two, and threw the pieces at her feet.

"Don't you ever hit me again!" I said.

And she never did.

We visited Aunt Thelma's and Uncle Don's cottage at the lake in Michigan every summer until I was 14. It was my favorite communion with Nature, when I was allowed to row their boat a little way along the shore to the magical lily-pads, all by myself. It always put me into a reverie that filled my heart. It was the intoxication of being outdoors in the fresh air, with the uneven feeling of sand underfoot instead of carpet, of my skin feeling silky swimming in the soft lake water, of listening to the birds and the breezes rustling through the tall trees, and the fragrance of it all; the outdoor fires with the marshmallows roasting, the dogs barking in the distance…and always the faraway drone of the motorboats along the wide expanse of the lake. All my senses were awakened, which was so wonderfully foreign to me. And best of all was being able to row alone along the shore and drift among the lilies, just being. These are the memories I keep returning to the most.

In the evenings, my parents and Aunt Thelma and Uncle

Don would leave me alone in the cottage while they went to the Ramona, a local dance hall for the evening. This lake was near Chicago in the era of the Big Bands of the 1940s and '50s and in the summer even the most famous ones toured all over Michigan playing the fabulous music of the Great American Songbook at the dance halls at all the lake resorts. I didn't mind being alone. I listened to the radio station broadcasting all that wonderful music I already knew and loved from *Your Hit Parade* on the radio, and it was so exciting to hear it coming live now from the ballroom of a hotel in Chicago. Along with those songs I loved, I could hear murmurs of the people laughing and talking and clinking their cocktail glasses together. I imagined how that would feel when I was grown up when, just like in the movies I'd be dancing to this music, dressed in a beautiful gown and living a happy, sophisticated life.

When I was in high school and dating, I shared my dreams with my mother of one day becoming a wife and mother myself. I was drying the dishes she was washing.

"One day, I'll be washing dishes for my own family," I said, dreaming that scene.

My mother said nothing, only making a sound that seemed to scoff at the idea of my falling in love and marrying. Of course, I thought she meant it as a criticism; that somehow, I wasn't "marriage material". Now I wish I had known what she was thinking about her own marriage and how she felt about being a mother. It might have given me a dose of life's realities, beyond the romance of it all. Would it have helped? Would I have believed her? Would I even have listened?

Then came a day when I felt like I'd stepped into another life. I was 16 that summer, and my mother had signed me up to take life drawing classes at the local college-level art school downtown. I was glad that she must have noticed that I was interested in drawing people and felt that I had some talent for it.

On my first day of class I was stunned when the lady who had been sitting on a small, raised platform and chatting with the teacher, suddenly stood up, dropped her kimono and assumed a pose. She wasn't even wearing underwear. I never dreamed we would be drawing naked people.

I felt shy to stare at her, but all the other, much older students acted like it was no big deal and began to sketch, after first sharpening their charcoal sticks on small sandpaper pads. I had those items too, so my mother must have taken the bus downtown to the school to get them for me. Watching the others, I learned how to use them. We were each straddling our own small bench with our large drawing pads propped up against the board at the front end. It turned out that this was the best training for me to learn anatomy instead of drawing people from my imagination. And it served me well as the foundation for my later development into becoming a professional fashion artist. After my initial shock of being invited to stare at naked people wore off, I loved it.

One morning I was about to leave to catch the bus for school. My father was home on vacation, and my parents were sitting together out in the sun in the back yard, chatting and drinking their coffee. I called out through the screen door to tell them I was leaving to go to school.

My mother called back, "Would you rather go to New York?"

What? WHAT?

Of course, I had told them of my dreams of one day going to New York, and they knew about my passion for the movies, but I could never have dreamed this. It was an invitation beyond my imagining. I was ecstatic! They even told me I could take a friend with me. Within hours my friend Marcia arrived and by late afternoon that day we were all packed into our big white Buick for my father to drive us all the way there. I was sure that New York was full of miraculous adventures, just awaiting my discovery.

We spent one night in a motel on our way there, and I couldn't stop giggling at this outrageous and completely unexpected adventure my parents had created. Maybe my mother was happier now for some reason. She hadn't been as critical of me since I'd started high school. That made me happier too, and now I was giddy.

We arrived after dark so my first sight of the city was dazzling, just like I knew it would be from the movies. I was in awe, with my dream come to life. In person everything was far more enormous than I had imagined. The signs in Times Square with the flashing colored lights were almost too big to take in. I could have died of happiness right then.

My friend Patty was spending the summer with relatives in New York, and she had given me her phone number. I called her as soon as we got to our hotel. My parents had said that we three girls could all go out together on our own the following evening, so we made plans with Patty to meet us at our hotel the next afternoon. Imagine that today? But this was 1955, and either this was a more innocent time, or my parents simply didn't know what danger we might have been in. Either way, we didn't question it. We were just delighted to pretend we were grownup young women able to navigate easily on our own in this most sophisticated city.

After the other girls got into the taxi on our big night out, I stepped in backward, not noticing that there was extra spacious leg room, and that the seat was further back than where my bottom was aiming. I landed on the floor with my legs up in the air, with the crinolines we all wore under our summer dresses showing for all to see. It wasn't easy to get upright because I couldn't stop laughing.

"Please take us to Sardi's," I said to the driver, when I assumed a more confident position on the seat and managed to stop giggling. I had read that Sardi's was where all the Broadway stars went directly after the first night opening of a new show to read the reviews, and I simply had to get there. Patty and Marcia were glad to let me choose our itinerary.

Next, we went to Rockefeller Center for a tour of the NBC

television studios. And afterward, as we walked along Fifth Avenue, I had the feeling we might be close to the legendary Stork Club where I just knew we would see famous stars. And in the next block, there it was! We walked right to it, and in through the door where we were met by the maitre'd, who told us gently that we could not come in unescorted by a man. To ease our disappointment, he brought us ashtrays and matches for souvenirs. I promised him I would return someday with my escort in tow.

The next morning, Marcia and I began regaling my parents about our exciting adventure, and I'm sure we kept it up on our drive back, all the way home to Indiana. My parents seemed so delighted with my company and to be enjoying all the fun we were having. It felt so good to be this happy.

With all this as background, you can see that I was primed to search for a therapist. And more. I knew there was more. Though I hadn't the words for it then, eventually I learned that what I was longing for was even more profound than the answers I could find in therapy.

What I was longing for was a deeper spiritual connection than I had yet found.

Three
SPREADING OUT: Out of High School and Off to College 1956-1959

After that gift of going to New York, I knew that I would grow up and get out and never look back.

Senior year began that Fall, and honestly it passed in a blur. I know there were dates and dances and football games; there were slumber parties with girlfriends and hosted parties with boyfriends, the senior prom and graduation and "fun" but my eyes were already fastened on my far-away future, which was getting closer now.

In the meantime, there was college, and I could hardly wait to get away to live on my own in a dorm. The day I was putting my campus-bound trunk in my parents' car, my boyfriend came over to say goodbye. He was about to return as a sophomore to a Big Ten state university in Indiana, and I was bound for a small women's junior college in Missouri, not that far away.

I had chosen Stephens because it excelled in classes in the

arts, and even offered a course in fashion illustration, which I loved, and had already been studying in high school for the past three years. I was naturally attracted to the fashion art style, painting with flexible brushes that allowed me to effortlessly create elegant long black lines, thick and then thin, back and forth, as they traveled the length of a woman's long-legged figure on the watercolor paper.

None of the colleges or universities in Indiana offered any fashion or commercial art courses. I knew this opportunity would be important for me. Nevertheless, my going out of state to school was too much for my boyfriend.

"I'm going to break up with you now," he said. "Because my parents said that you're going to come back here all 'stuck up'!"

Such a quaint Hoosier synonym for "arrogant". Well, so long and thanks for the heads-up and especially for making more room in my life for real adventures! I laughed all the way to Missouri.

I majored in art and minored in drama, where I often shared scenes in acting class with Dawn Wells, who not much later became Mary Ann on *Gilligan's Island*. I loved my adventurous new classmates who had come to the college from all over the country. In the words of Jackie, one of my new chums: "Sherle, there are monuments to build and elephants to ride - and we want to be there when they saddle 'em up!" Now we're talking. My new friends wanted to talk about *life*.

We spent hours each evening in the "smoker" the one common study room where smoking and talking was allowed, imagining what our lives would become. We read *The Catcher In The Rye* aloud, feeling free and golden. This was a time of such innocence and full of possibility. I felt that everything was possible. And that my own true-life adventures lay just ahead.

Although I remember feeling generally happy and cheerful and full of potential during those two years at Stephens, when the boy I had been dating for several months broke up with me, I began to drop into a depression, feeling suicidal for the first time since I was a child. And one day I just walked off campus and out onto the highway leading out of this little town.

I hadn't gotten far beyond the city limits when I began seeing a lot of huge semi-trucks coming toward me. I wondered if it could happen so quickly that I would never even suffer if I just jumped out in front of one at the last possible moment.

It was a cloudy, overcast sky, threatening rain. A man driving a nice sedan pulled over on the shoulder near me and, leaning out the window, asked me what the matter was. Did I need help? Why was I walking out here? He said he was a sheriff's deputy and had been driving in the other direction when he saw me and wanted to check. He'd made a U-turn. He saw my tear-stained face. "Are you from one of the colleges?" he asked. "Let me take you back. This is dangerous for you to be walking out here."

He seemed like a genuinely nice person, not at all creepy - and so against every warning I'd ever heard since I was a child about not getting into a car with a stranger, I got in. He did not drive me back into town, but off the road and into the woods and stopped the car. He turned off the engine. I sat there looking down at my hands in my lap. Frozen. Terrified. I really didn't want to die. Not now. Not like this.

He hadn't touched me...yet. But I knew he was going to. I cried. I pleaded. I begged. "Please take me back. PLEASE." I couldn't look at him. He said nothing. How long did I keep this up? It must have been at least 15 minutes. It was a lifetime.

I never looked up. I just kept crying and begging him not to hurt me. Tears and snot ran down all over my hands. He said nothing. He started the car. Was he going to take me somewhere even more remote?

We were back on the highway, and then *Dear God* he was driving back into town.

He let me out at the edge of the campus, without a word.

I never told anyone. It was such a compassionate gift from God that it was beyond speaking of. How could I have been worthy of such deliverance when I had been ready to destroy the life God had given me?

The man who might have raped and killed me had saved me from ending my life myself.

Book Two: Performance

Four
DROPPING OUT: MEETING JACK, LEAVING SCHOOL, LIVING IN SIN 1959-1961

Somehow, I must have pushed that horror into the furthest reaches of my mind, because I was able to return to classes and get good grades and laugh with friends and go on dates and have fun again. I graduated, saying *let's keep in touch forever* to friends, though we all knew we'd probably never see each other again.

It wasn't hard to say goodbye because my vision was already back to where it had always been, focused on the wonderful adventures yet to come. I was on the lookout for a fascinating boy to take me there, a boy who had Been Places and Done Things.

I was now in St. Louis, newly enrolled in the art school at Washington University and I had already been developing enough skill to believe that art could be my ticket to someplace wonderful. I didn't know how exactly, I just trusted that it could, and that it would.

The first week of classes, I was in the university bookstore, absorbed in looking at a rack of books by my favorite author, Ernest Hemingway. A rakish-looking young man appeared beside me, and as if we were already having a conversation, he was telling me that he had a copy of a magazine, *The Paris Review*, featuring an interview with Hemingway. The questions were as interesting as the answers, he said. Did I want to meet him tomorrow and he'd share it with me? Yes! This was a young man, not a boy. Immediately I felt the electricity.

As he bounded toward the door, I called out my name. As if in stop-action, he paused, "Yes, I know!" He didn't mention his name, but he didn't have to. I was hooked.

The next day at noon, he appeared in an English sports car, a dark green 1953 MG convertible with the top down.

"Hi, I'm Jack!" he said, and motioned for me to get in the car.

He told me we were in the same 11:00 AM life drawing class. An artist too! Oh, I hoped he was a good one. I knew that life drawing was my forte, and it would be awkward if he weren't.

From the beginning, Jack carried an energy that made him seem like he was always in motion, tossing off a pithy remark on his way to some place fascinating. He'd throw you a glance. Might you be lucky enough to be invited along?

We sat there in the parked car with the top down, in the blazing noonday sun, while he read the article with the voice of the practiced raconteur that he was. I was enthralled. The other boys I'd known and dated faded far into the background. They were cute and fun but not exciting. They'd been about as intriguing as insurance salesmen to me. But Jack was the Real Deal, as I was about to find out. He *had* Been Places and Done Things, truly. He showed me his passport! And he told me his stories as if he were doing the voiceover on a documentary of his own adventurous life.

The following day we met for lunch again after our class and he took me to the apartment he shared with his mother. When we arrived, she was not at home, but in her absence someone else had visited. Three extraordinary oil portraits he had painted had all been slashed with a knife! I had never seen the results of an act of violence and felt sickened. Who would do such a thing? He said it must have been a girl he'd dated that he didn't want to see any more. I felt sicker. But I pushed it away.

I need not have worried about the level of his talent; these portraits were brilliantly painted. I was amazed at the level of his genius, and I couldn't wait to hear where he'd studied to learn to paint this well.

But first he told me about having recently returned from

Korea, where he was shot in the elbow and sent to recover in an Army hospital. He'd faked a psychiatric test so he could be discharged and sent home for being shell-shocked, instead of being sent back to the front. And with the GI Bill he was able to enroll in this expensive private university art school we attended.

(Ohh...he cheats, he lies, he manipulates the truth. But this is hindsight. I felt it, but I didn't want to see it then.)

My favorite story was the one that happened before that. When he was 16, and knew he would be drafted at 18, he begged his mother to give him the $500 his father had left for his college education so he could go to Paris, since he might possibly die in the Korean war. She was such a softie and of course she gave in and off he went. He told me how, for a year, he had survived by listening for American accents in tourist areas like the Eiffel Tower, then introducing himself and offering to take people to restaurants and bars in the bohemian sectors, Montmartre and Montparnasse, where they could see the *real* Paris, and of course, buy his dinner. I thought this was brilliant and so adventurous. I tucked away my tinge of misgivings about his having cheated on the Army's psych test.

And then he told me where and how he had learned to paint like that. Without the funds to attend classes at L'Ecole des Beaux-Artes, the art school of the Sorbonne, he simply set up an easel at the Louvre, and learned to copy Rembrandt's mysterious technique of layered glazes. Soon he began hanging out with other young artists and models and actors. I was breathless hearing Jack tell the story of how he met Ernest

Hemingway there, a man who also liked to drink and hold forth with all these young cafe habitués.

He claimed that Hemingway had said to one and all "If you're ever in Havana, stop by!"

So, years later, when he was living and painting in Chicago, and a patron wanted to pay Jack even more than the agreed upon price for one of his commissioned paintings, Jack said, "Just buy me a round trip ticket to Havana!"

He arrived in Cuba, located Hemingway's home, and jumping over the fence, found his way to the front door. Of course, Hemingway didn't remember him, but he was impressed with Jack's chutzpah, gave him a stiff drink, and put him up for a couple of days. Jack made several sketches of him, elegant life drawings he showed me.

Well! Of course, I was knocked out. Jack was good-looking in an intellectual, sophisticated way, two years older than I, an exceptional artist, a fascinating storyteller (I had to believe his stories were all true) and, it turned out, a writer too. And he'd lived in Paris! My dreams had only aimed as far as New York, because back in the 1950s I thought only millionaires could go to Europe.

How deeply was I hooked? So deeply that even though I soon admitted to myself that I didn't really like him, that he wasn't a very nice person, I didn't stop seeing him. I was mesmerized by his prodigious talents and exciting tales. And I ached to do the things he'd done, go to the places he'd gone, meet the kinds of people he seemed to know how to meet.

He was my first sexual experience, and though he wasn't a

tender or romantic lover, it was very heady stuff to be awakened in this new swirl of my own sexual energy. I told myself that I was staying with him because I thought I was supposed to marry him and have his child. And though many years would pass before I would hear people talking about reincarnation and karma and grow to understand it's meanings in my life, I'm sure this was my first inkling of a *knowing* of a karmic connection.

It would take me half a lifetime to learn what it was about him that kept me so enthralled, and in such discomfort. He was a narcissist. A term understood and talked about frequently now, but not then. And there was more. His energy was what I would much later learn to identify as very dark.

But I had no idea how relationships worked. Most of my experience had been trying to stay out of my mother's way, so there's the indication that I was already a complete people-pleaser. I know now that I had also been a little frightened. Still, this man fascinated me. It was a heady feeling, being in the proximity of his genius. It inspired me to do my own best work. Everyone else, by contrast, seemed dull and grey.

One Friday afternoon I was on the phone with Jack, standing in the hall at the dorm, when he told me that painting and writing would always come first for him, before our relationship. My world and my dreams instantly vanished. Gone. We hung up and I went into my room and swallowed a bottle of aspirin.

Then I got scared and phoned him back. He called an emergency number.

The policeman who sat with me in the ambulance was kind and consoling, telling me I'd be all right. It was a very different story in the hospital. While they pumped my stomach, a frightening procedure, the attending doctor was very angry.

"How dare you do this?" he hissed at me. "We're trying to save lives here, and you take up our time because you tried something awful and selfish like this?" I was shocked. I can understand the psychology of it now, but at the time it was painful not to have anyone care about why I had done it.

After they were through, they tied me to a gurney and left me in a hallway for a long time. No one came near me or even walked past me. It was several hours before they put me in a room.

Jack didn't come to see me until the next day. And he was angry too, and icy cold.

Before they discharged me on Sunday afternoon the doctor made an appointment for me with the university psychologist for the following day. At the appointment, this doctor asked me to describe my relationships with both of my parents. I told him my feelings and begged him not to tell them what I'd done. "It would kill them," I said. But I didn't believe that. I was just afraid they would take me out of school and away from Jack. And evidently, the school didn't notify them. Would it have helped me if they had?

Even though he had been so cold toward me about my suicide attempt, never even discussing it or asking me how I felt, Jack assumed we were still in a relationship. And I was relieved. I thought, given his chilling glances, that he was going to break up with me. Then where would I be? I already felt that I couldn't bear to lose him.

He rented a room for us in a rooming house near school, where the bathroom was down the hall, and talked me into leaving the dormitory. I had never imagined breaking such a rule. Just walking out. There was a bed check every night in the dorm. What would happen when I wasn't there? I couldn't let myself imagine it.

And where was I? I had never imagined even walking into such a dingy, forlorn place, let alone living here. I was helpless. I was under Jack's spell. Literally.

Because I was marked absent from the dormitory, I was reported to the Dean of Women and to the Dean of Art. My parents flew in from Indianapolis. My father tried to talk to me. I knew I was the age he had been when he married the first Dorothy. I didn't want him to go through the pain of telling me the awful mistake he had made at my age. I wouldn't listen. I left the room. After that, he didn't try to say anything to me for a long time.

The Dean of the Art School said that the Dean of Women would not let me live off campus, nor on campus. So I had to leave school, though he felt I was very talented and told me I could return in the Fall semester when the Dean of Women would be retired. In the meantime, he graciously made arrangements for me to finish out the Spring semester at the art school in my hometown. It was the same school where in happier days I had gone to summer school and first learned to draw naked people. My parents and I flew home. For the next few months, we barely spoke.

I was miserably adrift without Jack and even though I went to classes, I moved through the days like a zombie. I flunked out. On the last day of school, my mother drove me to the bus station, and I left on a bus an hour later to go back to visit Jack. I never returned.

Hours later when I arrived in St. Louis I called my father, asking him to ship my clothes to me. When the trunk arrived a week later, I sobbed. This was the trunk that had held everything I'd taken with me to my first year at Stephens, when I was still a nice girl who got good grades, when my parents were still proud of me. I'd been so eager for adventure. Well, I had found it. Now I'd cut my ties to my parents and I was finally on my own, frightened and totally unprepared to be a grownup.

Jack had a little bit of money from a car accident settlement, and he rented an apartment for us. He drove a taxi part time and began writing seriously. I got my first job as a fashion illustrator in a large downtown department store, drawing women's clothes for the advertisements in the newspapers. I was thrilled to become a professional artist. It was St. Lous, not New York. But I was a pro, at last.

The day soon came when my first drawing appeared in the newspapers for everyone to see! I was so proud. That evening after work, I got on the trolley to ride home, and there on the trolley floor was a discarded newspaper with the page graced with my drawing on top – and people were stepping on it as they walked to their seat. When I told my friends about that at work the next day, a seasoned advertising copywriter just laughed and said, "Our work wraps tomorrow's fish!"

I felt an overriding shadow of sadness about my ruined relationship with my parents. And I had no idea how to find peace with myself over what I had created.

But I found such joy during the day at work. Somehow, I could push the sadness aside because I was excited to be drawing and painting for a living, and because I always had such fun with Dodie, another artist who worked with me who had become my newest, dearest friend. She called me "Squirrel" because it rhymed with Sherle.

Each day on our lunch hour we would leave the advertising office and dash through the department store, beginning on the street floor at the makeup and perfume counters, sampling the newest delights. Next, we'd ride the escalator to the second floor, where we tried on lots of hats, much to the amusement of the older saleswomen who seemed to think we were young and adorable. And then, our favorite: we rode all the way up to the Fur Salon where we would close our eyes and try to guess whether we were touching the unbelievably soft chinchilla fur or just the air. Those saleswomen on that floor never let us try on anything.

One evening at 5:30, as we were about to leave work for the day, we were walking past the gift wrap area. It was Christmastime and there were several people standing at the counter. I looked down at the floor and saw a $20 bill lying there, not anywhere near the gift wrap counter, or any other counter. I picked it up and showed it to Dodie. We sat down on a nearby bench and waited to see if anyone came along, appearing to be looking for it.

After several minutes, when no one did, we claimed it as ours! Giggling with joy at our unexpected fortune we ran out the door and across the street to Walgreens drug store, where we sat at a little table and ordered grilled cheese sandwiches and chocolate malts! There has never since been a meal as magical as this one was for me. Dodie and I didn't earn enough to "eat out" – we had to bring our lunches to work, always. Our salary was only $50. @ week, and the take-home pay barely more than $35. After our supper we still had $14 left to split, so we went back to the store, which was open late for holiday shopping and we bought handsome sweaters as Christmas gifts for our boyfriends.

It was 1959, and in the parlance of the time, Jack and I were living in sin. I felt embarrassed not to be married. I couldn't even tell Dodie or my other girlfriends at work because in those days I imagined that only trashy girls would live that way, and I still thought I was a good girl, despite everything I'd done to hurt my parents by dropping out of school and abandoning the expensive education they'd already paid for.

My mother accused me in a letter of having had an abortion, which wasn't true, would never have been true, because I wanted a baby so much. I phoned my father at his office and told him how much that had hurt me. For her to even think that of me paused our correspondence for a long time.

I had no one I could confide in or go to for advice. And if I'd been awake and aware, I would have known that I needed it badly.

Jack was mentally, emotionally, and sexually abusive. He was cruel, actually, though I was unable to identify those qualities then. His extraordinary talent at everything he touched, including painting, writing, telling stories, even building a wall of bookcases in our apartment, and then spending months crafting an enormous model of an historic three-masted sailing ship, was hypnotic to watch unfold.

But finally, though, after nearly three years together, I was hurting enough to call for a taxi to the train station. I ran down the stairs of our apartment building as I heard Jack yelling, asking me what was going on. The taxi drove up and I jumped in, but Jack jumped in his car with our little Beagle puppy and followed us. He bounded into the train station, looking stricken at my departure, carrying our puppy and begging me to stay. He had never shown me that much attention, and I so badly wanted to believe he loved me and wanted me that I gave in. Then I immediately felt sick, knowing I'd let go of that one shred of strength and power I'd held so briefly. I was back in Jack's darkness, and the shadow of sadness returned.

Rather abruptly one morning, a few months after that episode, as I was putting on my lipstick and getting dressed for work, Jack told me he had just had a dream of going to Europe to buy an ocean-going boat, sailing it back to the States, and chartering it. He said he was going, and I was to follow when I had $500 saved to bring with me, as well as the money I would need for my passage. Now as I'm writing this, I see that $500 then would be $5000 today.

A determined young man of his word, Jack left soon after to follow his new dream. Off he went, with the portable typewriter my parents had given me for my high school graduation tucked under his arm; the one I later found he had hocked in New York before leaving on the ship. Of course, I let him take it; I thought he needed it because he was a serious writer.

Within a few weeks, he sent a letter saying he had wound up in Oslo, Norway where he found "Cutlass," a boat for sale that was nearly 100 years old, having been built in 1865 for the King of Norway as a racing sloop. It had been tied up and only used as a party boat in the Oslo harbor for 20 years. Even so, it still had a strong hull, and only needed all new rigging. He had already bought it and begun learning how to navigate with the help of his new English friend, a veteran sailor named Paul Johnson.

Later letters reported that, with Paul as guide, they had sailed the boat and landed in northern Holland. Paul went back to England, while Jack spent the winter living on the boat, working on repairs from a bad storm they'd endured. And nearly dying of pneumonia, he said, during the bitterly cold days and nights on the North Sea coast there.

I was so eager to join him, that of course I did as I was told, putting aside every dollar I made.

It would be my first chance at a real adventure. But when I had saved almost enough money, working two jobs and living rent-free with his mother, Jack sent a cable saying that he had a fire on the boat; his wallet had been in the jacket that he had used to beat out the fire, which had then caught fire itself. He'd thrown the jacket overboard with the wallet still in it.

Did I mention that he was a writer? Yes, I did. Did I believe him? No.

Did I want to get to Europe? Of course, I did. You bet.

So I sent Jack the money I'd saved and set out to save another $500 plus the cost of my one-way passage to join him.

Five
Waiting it Out: Working Two Jobs 1961

Here's the problem with not living in the present moment when your heart is set on a goal and your focus is always on the future: you don't know what you have, until it's over and gone.

If only I'd realized then, what fun I was having while I was having it. Learning to be present has taken me years. My eyes were always on the horizon.

So, while all my thoughts and every dime I could earn were now pinned on the moment I could join Jack in Europe, I failed to notice how much happier I was in those six long months, working at the two most wonderful jobs I could have imagined.

By now I had left my job at the department store where I was a fashion illustrator and was learning new skills as a layout artist at an art studio owned by two partners, both young married family men. They were terrific guys, friendly, kind, helpful and they each had a great sense of humor. Jim and Don were never condescending toward me, which was unusual in 1961. Even women who were full-fledged art directors, let alone beginning layout artists like me, were not allowed to become members of the St. Louis Art Directors Club. Advertising was 'man's work', exactly as it was portrayed in the popular television series *Mad Men* which set Episode One opening in 1960, the very year I had landed my first job at the department store.

Both partners at my studio were gifted artists who painted popular advertising illustrations of happy people enjoying picnics and other leisurely family activities, usually while drinking a famous beer. The art was printed and enlarged to appear on billboards across the country for many national clients. It was an incredible art education watching them work.

To get to this delightful job five days a week, I took a streetcar, then transferred to a bus to reach the studio, which was in a suburb. It was quite a schlep and then I had to do it all over again to get home. But I was very young, the days were such fun, and I was learning a lot.

They were good to me. Why didn't I notice then how much more fun it was to be in conversation with them, even just being in a room with them, than it was to be with Jack? Why did I still think Jack was the prize?

Knowing I had to make more money so I could get to Europe sooner, I found an additional job, this one as a cocktail waitress working six nights a week at a venue so extraordinary that a book was later written about it. The Crystal Palace was owned by Jay Landesman, a man I'd seen pictures of, but never met. I'd heard that his wife Fran had become a well-known jazz singer and songwriter, who wrote the lyrics to a song I loved, *Spring Can Really Hang You Up The Most*.

Forty years later I heard her perform that song at Joe's Pub in New York, and as I was leaving, I recognized Jay waiting in the foyer. I told him how much I had loved those months I worked at the Crystal Palace all those years ago. He was a very old man by then, leaning on his cane. My remark brought tears to his eyes, and to mine too, recalling the joy of those days, when I was so happy, getting ready for my big adventure.

Jack's dear mother Helen had invited me to live with her, and treated me like her own, not letting me pay her rent. She wanted me to be able to save money so I could get to Europe as soon as possible. I felt she had a sense that Jack was always up to something and thought that I would be a good influence on him. But Jack did all the influencing. He would soon become my first big test in learning to stand up for myself. I wish I could say I was a quick study. But no. I had miles to go.

To help me work these two jobs, Helen would always have supper ready for me when I got home from the art studio. She spoiled me with her made-from-scratch chocolate-chip-pecan cookies. Whenever she baked them, she would open the kitchen door to the fire escape, and an old one-eyed squirrel would hop on in and wait. He would never run off with the cookie she handed him but stand there holding it carefully with his two tiny hands, nibbling away quietly like a polite dinner guest. Helen told me he'd been a visitor for quite a while, and I could see they were old friends. How we loved watching him.

I've memorized moments like that since I was a child. They're like leafing through an inner scrapbook, so vivid that they feel like a time-warp I can always revisit at will. I can enter unseen and watch, but I can't change anything. The past is past.

Back to my tale. As soon as I finished supper, I changed into my cocktail waitress attire - a white shirt, black tights and a short black skirt with a black apron. Then I would lie down for a ten-minute power nap. Helen would wake me in time to add my lipstick and then off I would dash to the streetcar again, only not so long a ride, and this time I wouldn't have to transfer to a bus.

The Crystal Palace was in a bohemian neighborhood near downtown, called Gaslight Square, surrounded by artist's lofts and jazz clubs. I loved that atmosphere and now I was working at the best place of them all! It was a jazz club, a place to go dancing, and my favorite, a cabaret theatre that featured famous headliners like the young Barbara Streisand and Woody Allen.

As you entered the long first room, there were two bars to the left. The first one served customers and the far one was a service bar where the waitresses picked up the drinks to take into the cabaret theatre. On the right side against the wall as you entered, across from the two bars, was a row of petite old

European wrought-iron elevator carriages, fitted inside with a small table and two chairs, creating an intimate little booth. I thought it was the most creative and elegant idea ever.

Further down, past the service bar on the main floor, the door to the cabaret theatre was to the left and the jazz room to the right. Downstairs in the Rathskeller, a DJ from an FM radio station would interview visiting celebrities, which is where I met author James Michener shortly after reading his book *Tales of The South Pacific*. When I gushed with praise and told him I wanted to go there, he said, "Well, you'd better take a man with you, there aren't that many there!" To which I confidently replied, "Oh I already have a man!" Fingers crossed.

In the summer months when I first began working, there was also a large outdoor garden area with a live band and a smooth concrete dance floor. There were several more of those wrought-iron elevator carriage booths and a service bar at the back. My favorite bartender knew I didn't like strong drinks, so he would make me a creme de menthe grasshopper when I worked outside.

I quickly learned to have only a sip, once I'd stumbled a little carrying a tray of drinks making my way across the gravel floor of the outdoor garden.

That autumn the Jazz Room was turned into a Twist Room because Chubby Checker had just made the Twist a new dance sensation. Lessons were given and drinks were served. I really preferred the jazz, so I was glad to be promoted to serving drinks in the cabaret theatre. That meant that as soon as I served the first round I could sit down and watch the show, since no drinks could be served again until intermission.

It was exciting to be able to watch Phyllis Diller perform two shows a night and three on Saturdays, all month long that December! She was new to her fame then and seemed to be having a fabulous time. Offstage she was very funny too. She employed a slim and serious-looking young man who wore owlish glasses and dressed in a pinstriped suit. He sat on a straight-back chair in a corner of her dressing-room, holding a tiny notebook, jotting down the witty remarks she made to her guests as she held forth, which she would later write into her act.

Since her dressing room was adjacent to the area where we waitresses could change clothes or freshen up, sometimes I would have a chance to talk to her after the shows. I told her I was saving money to go to Europe and get married. She told me that she had never been there and was eager to go to Europe too, but now she was booked up for the next five years, so Europe would have to wait.

She got such a kick out of showing me her costumes hanging on a pipe rack…including the ones that were already becoming legendary when she was on television – like the orange and yellow horizontally striped ostrich feather dress. It was fun to see how thrilled she was with them. She pointed out:

"Look! Even my underpants are lined and custom-fitted with a zipper and *darts!*"

She was just a darling.

Thirty-five years later, I heard she would be appearing at the

Dallas Opera in *Cinderella & The Ugly Stepsisters*. After reading in the paper which hotel she would be staying in, I left her a note along with a little watercolor sketch of her. Later she left me a note telling me she remembered me, but who knows. The nicest thing is that she was gracious enough to say she did. She told me to come backstage after the show, so we could catch up! But after the performance, when I went to the stage door, I was told she had just left in a limo and I left the theatre, sorry to have missed her.

A week later I had a lovely letter from her, thanking me for reminding her of those early years of her career when she'd first hit it big, and saying she was so sorry I'd been told she'd left the theatre. It wasn't true, she'd been waiting for me! I told you she was a darling.

At the Crystal Palace, we weren't paid a salary; we just worked for tips. If we made less than $8.00 during our five-hour shift, the management would pay the difference. Can you imagine? Of course, that would be like $80 in today's money, still peanuts. But the time I spent at the Crystal Palace was pure gold. I would have paid them.

When we signed out from work at 2:00 AM the streetcars were no longer running, but Cathy, a waitress who had a car, would drive me home. So hungry after being on my feet for five hours (after a full day at the art studio), I was so glad she would always stop at a White Castle. We would sit in the car, eating cinnamon rolls and drinking hot black coffee while Cathy would tell me about her boyfriend, who was still in prison. From the Palace to the Castle. I loved every minute.

That was my life for the first three months until the cable arrived about the fire on the boat - and then I knew it would take me at least another three months before I could save another $500. I was horribly disappointed and not believing Jack's story, but there was nothing to do if I still wanted to go - but keep on. And I did want to go. Jack had promised me that he would marry me at last.

And finally, three months later, just as I'd hoped and prayed for, came the day when I was ready to leave Helen, the art studio, the Crystal Palace, and St. Louis, forever.

I said goodbye to all those kindnesses and all of that fun.

Six

STEPPING OUT: INTO THE WORLD, AT LAST 1962

I flew to my parents' home to say goodbye. They tried gamely to be cheerful, giving me a little wedding shower, inviting a few of my old friends from high school I hadn't seen in years. They even had my picture published in the Sunday newspaper on the front page of the section that told of upcoming weddings, something I had always dreamed of during those years when I was so shamefully living in sin.

On our last evening together, we went out to dinner at a quiet little café in the neighborhood. I told them I'd probably be gone for 20 years, and there wasn't a wet eye among the three of us. Not even from my Daddy. They were both in their fifties then, so I really felt that I was leaving them forever. It never occurred to me then that they might need me when they got older. With only one set of grandparents living in Michigan, whom I'd seldom seen, I'd never spent time with old people. I hadn't a clue.

Remembering that evening now, my announcement seems incredibly cruel. But at the time, I felt my parents were resigned to my going. And probably relieved; they had done all they could. I knew I had deeply disappointed them, though no words of reproach were spoken. That alone made me feel they were through with me. And really, who could blame them? But I was so caught up in having this adventure that I was sure would be magnificent, I didn't even let myself imagine how they might be hurting.

Nor did I realize what a dreamworld I was living in. I'd always wanted my life to be exciting, like the movies. Looking back now, I feel ashamed of my callous disregard for their feelings, but at the time, I could only feel my own longing to go after the wonderful life that I knew was waiting for me out there in the world.

The following morning, I tried to shrug off the familiar shadow of sadness I felt about my last night with my parents. I only wanted to feel excited and happy and to think about the details of the adventure I was beginning. Within hours, I would be leaving on the train for New York to board the *Queen Elizabeth*, the enormous ship that would take me across the Atlantic Ocean in only five days to Southampton, England. From there I would take the train to London, and later that evening, with the instructions Jack had given me on a crackling transatlantic phone call which I took in my mother's kitchen, I would board another train to Harwich on the Northeast coast of England where I would get the ferry to cross the English Channel – and finally meet him the following morning at the Hook of Holland, the port in Holland, near the port where he lived.

An ocean crossing can be quite relaxing in beautiful weather, with the fresh breezes coming off that gorgeous expanse of blue kissing your cheek… but in January on the grey Atlantic, the ocean is a roiling monster spitting ice in your face if you can manage to get the door open to go out on deck in the frigid temperatures. Mostly I stayed below deck, way below in the cheapest cabin I could book, shared with two women I'd never met. Thankfully, there was a small sink in the cabin, to get a glass of water or brush your teeth. But the toilets and the bathtubs were quite far down the hall.

It was only $150 for a five-day crossing including all your meals if you weren't too seasick to eat them and if you could get to the dining room, what with this gigantic ship pitching so much side to side that it was impossible to navigate your steps without holding on to the ropes running the length of the ship on both sides of the hallways. You had to hand-over-hand it down to the dining room entrance, finishing with a quick dash across an open space and praying to reach a chair without falling down first and sliding on your bottom across the floor. By the time I landed safely in a seat, all appetite was lost. Each time I made it there I could only manage to pocket an orange to take back to my room. I'm certain that 5 oranges in as many days was my total food intake. No scurvy here.

I barely remember one of my cabin-mates; I'm not even sure she spoke English. We had virtually no contact as I remained in my upper bunk, turned toward the wall (the bulkhead), trying to sleep through the awful dizziness that seasickness caused in me.

On the fourth day we saw land. It was too quiet, something was missing. I know! Where was the soundtrack? This was such a momentous event! I had to laugh at how the movies had conditioned me to expect music to accompany my adventure.

I thought we were looking at Southampton, England, where I would get off, but someone said "No, it's France!!" I was so beside myself with excitement to see Europe with my own eyes, that I must have squealed long and loudly. I piped down when I heard someone ask, "Is she getting off here?" and someone else answered, "Let's hope she is!!" Well, only one more night to get through and I would finally disembark.

The blessed day arrived - and I was ecstatic! I made it through Southampton customs with my baggage, including a raft of sea charts Jack had told me to buy for him, and I boarded the train for London. Through the window I watched England unfold before my wide-open eyes! We passed a small winding river with two swans floating on it...like a picture-postcard. Then as we got closer to London, more than once I saw angry-looking graffiti on large dark buildings "Stop Coloured Immigration". I'd never seen graffiti and the energy in it was frightening.

One of the women who had shared my cabin was on the train with me. We both had a free day to explore the city before we made connections to go further, so when we came into the train station, we checked our bags in lockers, found an American Express information desk and booked a day-long tour.

What a great time we had, riding a red double-decker bus with lots of other tourists, checking off all the London must-sees! We went first to the Tower of London, marveling over the case full of the glittering Crown Jewels, then shuddering at the marked site where Anne Boleyn's head was said to have bounced. When we arrived at the immense Tate Art Museum, I was thrilled to find my favorite artist's work, John Singer Sargent's magnificent painting "Carnation, Lily, Lily, Rose" which I had studied in art school.

Next, we marveled at the architecture inside and outside St. Paul's Cathedral, rode past the familiar sight of Big Ben, walked wide-eyed into the grandeur of Westminster Abbey, and rode around Piccadilly Circus and busy Trafalgar Square. As we wound through the streets, we noticed a very old-looking restaurant, Ye Olde Cheshire Cheese (rebuilt after the Great Fire of 1666, we later learned) and decided to go back there for dinner when the tour ended.

When we arrived, we were seated on old, burnished benches

at what looked like ancient tables with initials and long-ago dates carved into them...feasting at last (after only oranges for nearly a week) with a magnificent roast beef and Yorkshire pudding. I was so hungry, for food and for this marvelous adventure. At last, I was living the reality of a dream coming true for me.

Checking my watch, I realized I still had time to go to the theater because my ferry crossing to Holland didn't leave till two in the morning, and the train ride to take me to the ferry didn't leave until after midnight. So, saying goodbye to my companion, giddy with excitement and unafraid to be alone in a new country, I bought a ticket to see *My Fair Lady* on stage in the West End, which I found is to London what my beloved Broadway is to New York. The show was divine, and seeing it in the city of its setting was magical. I pinched myself! I was on my own and figuring out *Life*, and for that day and evening I felt exactly like those confident, radiant, young women in the movies!

After the show I hailed a taxi and got back to the station, retrieving my bags from the lockers. The train ride to Harwich was comfortable and soon I would be on the last leg toward my long-awaited destination. After sleeping overnight on the ferry in a little cabin, I would finally see Jack tomorrow morning at ten.

Seven
Turning Out: Holland/England 1962

Oh- when I caught sight of him there, *right there*, on the other side of the Customs partition, I began waving and hollering, "Jack! JACK!!" And when I got through to the other side to touch him, I threw myself into his arms, and cried and cried! *Which, I'm beginning to notice, seems to be my signature reaction, whether I'm happy, sad, frightened, or thrilled.* I couldn't stop; my relief was overwhelming. The fact that I was finally HERE was too huge to take in. I was awed at what I had done; all the work, all the money I had saved, all the effort and time and travel and seasickness and courage it took to be on my own like this in the world! It's what I had wanted my whole life, but still it was a scary undertaking, and I had *done* it!

For the first time ever, I was proud of myself. I knew then

that I really did have what it would take to keep making my dreams come true.

I tried not to notice that Jack wasn't as excited to see me, as I was to see him. What he did love was that my arrival reflected on him as a terrific romantic story that any audience would love. And Jack always had an audience. So he faked it well enough for others, conveying the impression that he was glad I'd arrived. But I knew he was not overjoyed like I was. I pushed that aside because I wasn't going to let it diminish my own excitement. I could literally feel that my eyes were wide open and beaming.

My very first evening in Holland, Jack and I were invited to dinner at the home of a couple who'd met him after reading in the newspaper about his winter sailing exploits, which they found fascinating. When they sought him out, and heard his tales in his own words, they fell under Jack's spell, just as I had.

Thea, the wife, welcomed me with a fragrant potted blue hyacinth, my first example of the warm hospitality of the Dutch. She told me she was so glad that I'd arrived that day so she could meet me before leaving the following morning for the Dutch East Indies to visit her sister.

I took off my winter coat, then quickly felt how cold and drafty the room was. There was no central heating, only heavy floor-to-ceiling woolen drapes to defend against the freezing cold weather. There was a wood-burning stove at the far end of the room, quite a distance from the table where we sat down for dinner, and I tried to keep my teeth from chattering.

Needing to use the bathroom but too shy to say so, I said I'd like to wash my hands. I was led to a sink that was all alone in a tiny room by itself. So now I had to ask, "May I use the toilet?" My first day in Europe, and I had much to learn.

Our hosts explained that they lived in a shared house with another family living on the other side of a large kitchen. Land was so precious in the Netherlands that it took years of waiting on a government list before people were able to acquire a single-family dwelling. They told us that when a couple becomes engaged, they sign up for housing, and by the time their first child is born they will probably be able to find living quarters. In the meantime, they will have to live with family members. This couple had no children, so they were not allowed to buy or rent a larger home, even though they were financially very well off. Still, they could afford other luxuries like the distant trip Thea was about to take.

Everywhere we went the Dutch people were so warm and inviting; they even insisted we smoke their cigarettes when we were in their home and save our own. Of course, we were all smoking back then, in 1962.

When we visited Jack's other new friends, they also insisted that we take advantage of using their showers, since we had none on the boat. I was grateful for the offer; something I'd always taken for granted had truly become a luxury. I was happy too that their home had central heat.

When we arrived there, the husband started to open the

stereo to remove the record they'd been listening to and replace it with someone singing in English. I said, "Oh, please don't change it! I love listening to the woman singing in French even though I don't speak the language!" I felt like I had landed in another dimension, finally arriving in Europe, and I wanted to be completely immersed.

The *Cutlass* was a very narrow boat built for racing on an afternoon, not built for living aboard, so the quarters were very small. I inched down the few steps to go below. As I entered, the first item was the galley, where I would cook, immediately to my right. It was the width of my shoulders and only deep enough to accommodate one large pan. Next to it was the main "salon" that was about the width of me with my arms outstretched to my left and my right. There was a battened-down table and built-in seating for two. Just beyond that, on both sides of the mast that filled the middle of the aisle, were very narrow bunks, just barely large enough for two people to lie very closely together. The only heat available was from a small smelly portable kerosene heater.

Not a very comfortable place to spend the days in, so while Jack worked on the boat, mending sails and replacing some of the rigging that had been damaged in the storm before I'd arrived, I would visit an American family who'd taken an interest in him, then in me, and invited me over. They were a delightful couple with five energetic children ranging in age from 3 years old to 18. The youngest two, at 3 and 5, spoke fluent Dutch and laughed out loud at being able to keep secrets from the grownups who didn't know what they were saying. The 7- and 10-year-olds spoke it well enough to go to a Dutch school, but the 18-year-old had to go to an American school.

Stan, the father, worked for Shell Oil and often drove on short afternoon business trips to nearby Amsterdam, Rotterdam, and Delft. He offered to take me along so I could enjoy the museums and cafes while he was busy with meetings. His wife, Betsy, spent her days baking bread and cooking meals for her growing family. I probably should have spent more time with her and learned to cook. But I was enthralled with all I could see in the cities and took Stan up on every offer to go.

By now it was early March, nearing the end of a cold gray winter. We had already spent two months waiting for the weather to change enough to make it possible to cross the English Channel. We were moored at the pier in Scheveningen, a fishing port, the sea harbor of the Hague. Here in the Netherlands, it was still bitter cold, and I was still missing American central heating. These Dutch were a hardy lot.

When Jack thought it began to look possible to set sail soon, he sent a cable to his English friend Paul, the veteran sailor who had taught him so much on the trip from Oslo to

Holland in autumn, telling him he really needed his help now to cross the Channel. Thankfully, Jack knew that I would be nearly useless as crew. He was going to need another man, someone who was very strong; not to mention, someone who knew a lot about sailing. Jack was learning on the job. Because this boat was 49 feet long and built for racing, he said that it ran very fast, and strength and experience were mandatory. Thank heavens Jack had learned that much and knew I had neither.

Paul cabled back: *"It is the middle of the winter."*

Came Jack's reply: *"I know"*.

Two days later Paul arrived on deck, calling down to us below, "You've gone right 'round the bend. You're mad as a hatter, wanting to sail in the winter, so I thought you might need a hand. What have you got to drink?"

Just the day before there had been increasing gale-force winds, and while we were warming ourselves with steaming cups of cocoa at a restaurant on the beach, I'd watched opened car-doors snap off their hinges and go flying across the sand.

When the wind had died down enough the next day, even in this still-freezing weather, the men determined we could set sail. We were headed for the village of Hamble in Hampstead, on the Hamble River in England, up from the tidal estuary Southampton Water. This was Paul's home base, where his parents still lived in Moody's Shipyard on the Yacht *Escape* where they'd raised him... and where he tied up his little boat *Venus* from time to time. But before we could get to Hamble, we had to make it down the coast to Belgium and then cross over to England at the Dover cliffs.

England was also where I hoped Jack would finally make an honest woman of me, after all those years of living in sin in St. Louis. He had told me before he left that we could marry when I got to Europe. Before I left the States, my father had strongly suggested that if he didn't marry me right away, I should take my money, go have a little holiday in Europe -and then come home. With $500 in 1962 money, that would have been more than possible. But of course, I had already signed over to Jack the entire $500 worth of American Express cheques I'd brought with me on the day I arrived, just as soon as he told me I must. And instead of listening to my father's advice, I obeyed Jack's dictum. I was unable to stand for myself. Or even try to negotiate. I was always at a loss to counter his demands.

Soon after we left the harbor, I became seasick and immediately thought, *This isn't fun or exciting, it's terrifying! Why would anyone choose to do this? More to the point - why had I chosen to be a part of it?* It had simply never occurred to me what this adventure might entail. I'd never been sailing before.

That first day we sailed down the coast of the Channel toward Belgium, and long after the night sky grew very dark, we sailed into a harbor at Ostende. We were moving far too fast and nearly crashed the boat into the pier, where we could see a crowd of people gathered. Women in ball gowns and men in tuxedos were staring in horror at the catastrophe they could see coming at them within seconds.

I have no idea how, but we stopped just short of disaster, pulled up and tied up. Into this elegant crowd I stepped, mortified to be seen wearing Jack's red sweatshirt with this message on the back: "U.S Olympic Drinking Team". The crowd that gathered around us thought we were a mirage; *no one* sailed in winter. This was a very fancy yacht club in whose basin we'd landed. Perhaps they gave us glasses of champagne, because the rest is a blur. But I know we slept that night on the boat, because for some reason I didn't understand, we weren't legally allowed to land. They could have just forced us away. But they must have taken pity on our craziness to sail in such weather. And it surely gave them a good story to tell.

We left the next morning for England, a much bigger adventure ahead. Having just crossed the Channel by ferry to get here two months earlier, I'd heard how rough these legendary waters are. This night, there was no moon. No stars. A bad thing, because Paul used a sextant to navigate by the stars. He and Jack both came down below deck where I was sitting, to pour over the sea charts and try to decide where we were, and how to proceed. Their conversation was getting intense, and Jack told me I had to go up on deck and 'man' the tiller, while they kept at their task. I'm sure Jack poured himself another brandy, leaving the figuring it out to Paul.

Up on deck, the night was pitch black. Freezing cold. *And wet.* Jack tossed me a stiff Army blanket, and I wrapped myself up as best I could. Then he hollered out directions, "Can you see that pinpoint of light in the far distance?" That was all I could see. I couldn't even see the mast a few feet beyond, although I knew about where it was.

"That's a lighthouse!" he yelled above the roar of the waves. "You *must* keep the mast to the left of that light, or we could hit the rocks along the coast!" Total novice that I was, I understood that warning immediately.

I couldn't believe how strong the current was and how difficult it was to control the huge wooden handle of the tiller. The surging waves kept trying to wrench it out of my hands. It was nearly impossible to hold onto, but desperately necessary.

Quick violent slaps of the icy salt water were stinging my face, burning my eyes. In the pitch blackness, the waves seemed to be coming from all directions, so there was no dodging it. Anyway, where could I have leaned if I could have seen it coming? I had to keep my eyes on that pinpoint of light or else.

With the constant churning waves tossing the boat, my stomach started churning too. I remembered Paul telling me his motto: "Never be afraid to be terrified!" And though I was horribly frightened, remembering this suddenly made me laugh. Laughing made me feel brave. I was proud of myself, facing this danger, holding tight to the tiller, doing what needed to be done.

How many hours did this go on? I have no idea. Eventually the men took turns on deck with the tiller, and I went below.

Adventures are *hard*. But I hadn't stopped to think they might be life-threatening. Still, somehow, I slept. Maybe I was finally adjusting to the motion and was rocked to sleep. I didn't wake until dawn when Paul called out:

"Look, Sherle! The White Cliffs of Dover!"

Eight
Finding Out: England, Married, Pregnant, Blind 1962

Seeing morning's light and calm water was great comfort after that terrifying night, though now I couldn't deny how out of my element I was. Realizing what a mistake I'd made coming here with my dreams of adventure, I had no idea how to correct it. I was just going to have to make the best of it, somehow.

Once we had crossed the Channel to Dover, the rest of the trip was smooth and we finally reached Paul's home base, the lovely little village of Hamble. It was everything I could have imagined an English village to be, like a drawing from a child's picture book come to life. There we tied up to the pier on a mud berth at Moody's Shipyard, floating when the tide came in, sitting on top of the mud when the tide went out.

Trying to figure out what I could do to "make the best of it", unable to imagine any other alternative, and finally screwing up my courage, I insisted to Jack that we get married. I was buoyed up by the feeling that I deserved it after all I'd done to get here, first cabling him $300 and then bringing him $500 more, and having been brave on that frightening crossing we'd just made.

Paul was all for it and recruited his parents to help make arrangements. Surprisingly, Jack went along with it, without protest. So, off we went to meet with the Vicar, who said he would "read the banns" for three weeks at his Sunday services, and if no one objected, he would marry us.

Then the Vicar explained how the ceremony would go, and announced that he would add a prayer for childbearing. Jack was not in favor of that detail, but I was elated and allowed myself a small squeal of delight. So over Jack's objections, the Vicar said, "There *will* be a prayer for childbearing!" I was thrilled and surprised. My wishes had never prevailed over his.

Oh, the red flags were flying. But they had been since the day we'd met, and I had never wanted to see them. At the time, I wouldn't have understood the concept, even though there was much about Jack that made me uncomfortable. But people didn't talk in such terms back then, at least, nobody I knew. I didn't understand that I was being manipulated; I believed I had made these choices on my own, and that now I had no further choice left but to keep going in the direction I'd set for myself.

The three weeks passed, flowers were gathered, and I wore the new blue wool suit I'd bought for the occasion. Paul's father and mother drove me to the wedding ceremony in their sleek dark blue 1937 Riley sedan to the magnificent ancient church in Bursledon, just down the river from Hamble. It had originally been built in the 11th Century and then remodeled in the 13th.

It seemed like a long service, and as I stood next to Jack in front of the Vicar, I felt fully the weight of this terrible mistake I had made. But now I had to get through this ceremony I had insisted on. Looking up at the Vicar as we knelt at the altar, I wondered how long it would be before I would be standing in front of a judge in a divorce court.

By this time, it was mid-April and warming just a little. To give you an idea of the temperature then, I was later wearing my winter coat at an outdoor gathering in Hamble during the afternoon on the fourth of July.

When we returned to Hamble from the church, all of Paul's local sailing friends and his parents and their friends, along with other international sailing couples who lived on their boats nearby, had gathered round to celebrate our wedding. There was much toasting to us and spreads of food all served on decorated tables outdoors. There were even wedding gifts! With a nod to my new domestic duties and the lack of electricity on our boat, I was given a kerosene iron to press our clothes, a little odd since we lived in sweatshirts and jeans, and an enormous pressure-cooker for the boat's tiny galley. It was sweet to be feted by this large group of assorted lovely people who had barely met us.

Jack got drunk and passed out on our wedding night. I was relieved.

Since I had never been very interested in the goings-on in the kitchen (always trying to stay out of my mother's way) I had brought along my *I Hate To Cook Book* (still available in a 50th anniversary edition on Amazon). The next day I tried my first recipe, an innocent-sounding little number that featured pieces of chicken, chunks of pineapple and two cups of rice dropped into my shiny new pressure cooker. Before much time had elapsed, there was pressure indeed, it totally exploded! Chicken and pineapple flew everywhere, while the rice stuck to everything within range: my clothes, my hair, and the floor of the boat.

At first, now that I was getting used to living this way, and we had made several new friends, it was kind of fun. A little primitive, living on a boat without plumbing, no toilet, no shower. But we had access to both at the Hamble Yacht Club. And for a while, we Americans were a novelty among the other boat people, who seemed to enjoy us. One wealthy American fellow was there, having an expensive boat built for him. He loved talking sailing with Paul and Jack, so he often treated the three of us to dinners at local pubs. Always, the bill of fare favored peas as the vegetable of the day, and Jack and I were getting a little weary of them. Paul never complained, and I did love watching him smash them on the back of his fork with his knife, in the English way.

One evening we came to a pub that was featuring Brussel sprouts.

"Please, I'll have the Brussel sprouts, thank you!" we all exclaimed together.

"Oh, I'm sorry," the waiter said, "we're all out of the Brussel sprouts, but we have peas!"

I was such a rube, fresh from the States. One day I went into the village to buy lettuce.

"Oh, it's not the season for lettuce, Luv!" I was told. And with all the ignorance of my (American) youth, I protested, "But there's never a season for lettuce!" I had so much to learn. Not just about vegetables, but about Life. It's not like the movies.

The day after our wedding, we newlyweds were invited to join Paul and some of his friends who were sailing down the coast for two weeks. This boat's length was 72 feet, far bigger and much more comfortable than Jack's. This was built for cruising, not racing. Going below I was astonished. There was an enormous main "salon" and beyond it a hallway with doors opening to individual cabins. Cabins! Not bunks.

Jack decided that we were going to quit smoking on that trip, so he brought along not a single cigarette. Quitting smoking is hard enough, but when it's not your own idea, it's ghastly. I was beside myself in withdrawal and angry with Jack. But I'd given him all my money, so I had no way to buy any cigarettes for myself. None of the others on this cruise were smokers either, so I couldn't even try to cadge one.

During that trip we were intimate for the first time in the four months since I'd arrived. And the Vicar's prayer for childbearing brought forth the results; within a month, I was pronounced pregnant at a free clinic I found when I took a bus down to Southampton.

What was I thinking, insisting that prayer be included when I was unhappy already? But this is what I'd wanted all my life, a child to love. And despite my misgivings about Jack, I felt blessed knowing that this soul had chosen me.

The next four months were awful. My morning sickness was so intense all day and evening long that the only things I could keep down were soda crackers and strawberries, and Paul was kind enough to keep me supplied with both. I saw very little of Jack. He was either working on some of the boat's rigging, mending sails, or drinking at the pub.

One afternoon, Jack and Paul had gotten a lift from a neighbor who had taken them into the next town to get a piece of equipment needed for the boat. Trying to forget about my upset stomach, I was looking around for something to read.

There were some paperback books, but none of them looked particularly interesting. I kept poking around and found a heavy book with a waterproof cover tucked under some papers on a small shelf. I took it out and saw the title: *Ship's Log: Cutlass: Oslo, Norway 1961*. Thinking this was probably just a technical record Paul had made on their trip from Oslo to Holland, with notations about the weather, the wind, and the measurements taken with his sextant, I started to slide it back onto the shelf. But then, for some reason, I decided to open it.

Jack had written in locker-room sexual detail about an affair he had been having with a Danish girl he'd met in Oslo, who'd come with him on this long sail to Holland. She'd stayed the past six months there with him, too. And he'd been having the time of his life with her. So this was why he'd lied to me, delaying me, telling me there had been a fire on board, and asking me to send him all the money I'd saved? Then telling me I couldn't come until I could bring even more? I felt sick.

It got worse. He wrote that Ellie had tried to kill herself when she realized I was coming after all, and he was dumping her. He noted how well he'd cleaned up the mess after she slit her wrists, first taking her to a doctor to get bandaged up, and then putting her on a train back to her parents in Copenhagen. I could see that he'd chosen me because I had some money coming for him. Ellie might have been great in the bunk, but she didn't have funds. It was all there. He didn't care, about either of us.

Suddenly I heard the sound of Jack's boots hitting the deck. He came below and saw me sitting there with the ship's log open on the table.

"What the hell are you doing with THAT?" he screamed. "That's none of your business! The ship's log is only for the captain to touch – and that captain is ME! Give it to me! NOW! And don't you ever touch it again!"

He tried to make me the villain for reading the ship's log, as if that were the wrong action here, not his infidelity, or her broken heart. It was such a familiar manipulation from him, but this time I didn't buy it. Now how was I going to keep "making the best of it"?

It should have been obvious to me why having a child was never a part of Jack's plans for himself. He began to talk of sailing across the Atlantic very soon in this narrow racing boat- certainly not built for any comfort at all. On his schedule I would be delivering the baby at sea. There was no way I could face that. So one morning I told him I was going to write to his mother to tell her I was pregnant.

"Oh, no – you're NOT!" He was so quick when he punched me hard in my stomach, that I never saw it coming. I ran off the boat onto the pier and into the village.

I kept running until I came to a thick deep forest where I could see beams of light coming through the tops of the tall trees. There were ferns of every height and ivy covering the forest floor.

Running a good way in, praying he couldn't find me, I finally sank face down onto this welcoming soft carpet of green. I was terrified. I sobbed soundlessly in case he'd followed me. Now the darkness I'd always sensed in him, but didn't understand, was evident. I felt he might even kill me. And I realized he was clever enough to get away with it. My parents had no idea where in the world I was by now. And he could tell the locals anything he wanted to, he could say that I'd gone back to the States to have the baby. That would make sense, they wouldn't question it.

Who he really was, was so obvious to me now. But what could I do? Where could I go?

Having had so little contact with my parents during those years I'd been living with Jack in St. Louis, and then with my latest cavalier departure, I felt I'd burned any bridges back to them. I lay there, reliving that last night before I left when we'd had dinner at that little café.

I remembered thinking that they seemed so emotionless as I told them I'd probably be gone for 20 years. I thought they had given up on me and wouldn't even want to hear from me, but now I knew they were my only hope to get away from Jack and protect my baby.

I lay there on the forest floor for hours, until the light was dimming. Terrified to return to Jack, but even more frightened of being in the dark all night, with whatever animals might find me, I finally stood up and made a run back to the boat.

Jack didn't hit me again and we barely spoke after that day.

Instead of writing to his mother, I cabled my parents, telling them I was pregnant and asking them to please wire me the money to come home. For weeks I waited for their reply, fearing they might never answer, might never forgive me for all the grief I had caused them.

At the Yacht Club that graciously allowed us the use of their facilities, I soaked in the bathtub staring at my toes, feeling afraid I wouldn't hear from my parents and feeling betrayed by Jack. What a mess I'd made of everything. I had really betrayed myself, not listening to my inner voice that had always known the truth, that Jack wasn't a good person.

The next day I walked up the hill to the tiny grocery, along the soft worn path, where beautiful little wildflowers grew along the edge. What a dear little village. At the grocers, as I was walking though the store with my cart, I began to feel slightly faint. When I got to the cashier, she asked me if I was all right, and when I admitted "Not quite," she invited me to sit down before I went back down the hill.

"Put your head down toward your knees, Luv" she said. And I did. But I was embarrassed to take up space on the chair in such a tiny place, when she had other customers, so after a minute I got up and reassured her I was much better now.

I carried my groceries in the soft cloth bag I'd brought with me and began retracing my steps back along the path, looking down at the pretty flowers at the edge. But there was something wrong. I could only see the colored outline of each tiny flower petal. The inside was white, or blank. I blinked. I looked at the grass. Each blade was outlined in green and inside was only white. And then I looked up, and across the lawn toward the Yacht Club I saw there were people walking, but they were just colored outlines too. Shy to do this but too scared not to, I called out to them for help! I heard one of them call my name. I couldn't tell if it was a man or a woman, but someone knew me. I hollered out "I can't see! I'm going blind!"

They all must have come to help. With someone on either side holding my arms, they guided me gently across the grass to step inside the Yacht Club's parlor. There they sat me down in a big leather chair and talked to me softly and reassuringly while my head was down, for over an hour when, thank God, my sight miraculously returned.

Nine

Looking Out: For Myself and My Baby 1962

My life has been fueled by my longing to love and be loved. Growing up with my critical mother, I ached for the warmth and closeness of being tenderly held. I thought that's what I could give to my child when I became a mother myself. So along with all those years of waiting and wanting to grow up and get out, came a continual longing to have a child of my own, to create the loving relationship I was hungry for, but in the opposite role.

Certainly, I would know how to be the mother. I had only to remember what I had wanted for myself as a child. Of course, I would easily be able to raise my own child with great loving care. I was sure that I would know exactly how to nurture and guide them, as I was certain I would grow in wisdom on our journey together.

When it finally happened, and I became pregnant despite Jack's wishes, I was so grateful. Even after finding the ship's log, even with the fear and disgust I now lived with, I was filled with awe that a soul had chosen me, had seen my loving heart, had felt that I was the one who would nurture them and hold them safely in the world.

Trusting this gave me the strength to know that somehow I could leave Jack, even though I was without a cent, living on a sailboat tied up on a river at a little village, somewhere in England.

As weeks passed and I still hadn't heard from my parents, I tried to think of other ways I could leave Jack and take care of myself and my baby. Feeling hopeful from having already worked as an artist in St. Louis, I wondered if I might be able to get a job and live in nearby Southampton, a big city where there would surely be opportunities. I was excited to imagine that I could escape this man who was not only emotionally abusive, but who had become physically terrifying to me.

Now I had an overwhelming regret for not honoring my original truth about him, when I first sensed that he was not a good person, that I didn't even like him, really. But he was boldly adventurous and I had just wanted to have fabulous adventures too. Well, now I was having them. And they didn't match my dreams for myself. Not at all.

I knew I had to get busy. If there was a chance to find work, first I had to create a group of sketches. When I told my idea to Paul, an artist himself, he helped me again, bringing me the art paper and watercolor paints and brushes I needed. I sat down on the narrow floor of the boat, trying to create beautiful fashion drawings from my imagination, without the reference material I was accustomed to having, like photographs of fashion models with ideas for poses, and details of clothing and accessories. I just winged it.

After I had painted several sketches, I tied them up into a little makeshift portfolio and, still feeling queasy with morning sickness, I rode on the upper deck of the double-decker bus for a dizzying 45 minutes through winding and hilly country roads before connecting to the highway that led into the city.

When I arrived in Southampton, I stepped into one of those red phone booths you see in English movies and rang up a few advertising agencies from the telephone book's business pages to see if they would grant me an immediate interview.

I desperately hoped I might somehow get a job that would let me stay in England and create a life for the two of us. Of course, I knew nothing about work permits or visas. I simply assumed a job would make it possible for me to stay in a foreign land and raise my child.

The men at two different ad agencies who were kind enough to give me an interview that afternoon both tried gently to tell me that there were no fashion accounts there, they were all in London, where they advised me to go. They said that all their clients in Southampton manufactured products for 'manly' trades: shipbuilding, furniture-making, and fishing equipment. No beauty here.

There was no way I could make it to London. It was too far away to make it a day trip. I had no money for transportation, food, or lodging. I had given it all to Jack. It was out of the question.

While I still hadn't heard from my parents, the other boat people in the village learned of my predicament, although I don't believe they realized Jack's frame of mind or the state of our marriage. They just knew that he was planning to sail the Atlantic and I needed a place to live to await the baby.

A dear man, known as the Skipper, invited me to come live with him and his wife and young son. I had met him during one of the outdoor parties held for the boat people and found him to be delightful. He'd had a little too much that afternoon of the local hard cider, and as he ambled toward me, somewhat unsteady on his feet, he said, "Not to mind, Luv! I'm just a wee bit tiddly!" He had complete charge of a very expensive yacht owned by a wealthy man, a legal bookmaker in London, who came down to sail it from time to time. The Skipper kept his boat polished and ready. He owned a small grocery and offered to let me work there and share his family's home in the back of the store.

How many times in my life have I looked back at that enormous fork in the road and wondered how my life and my child's and our relationship with each other might have changed if I'd made that choice! Ah, the road not taken.

The next day my parents cabled the money I'd asked for. So, I declined the Skipper's kind offer and booked my passage, set to leave the following week. Suddenly, it was all happening very fast. After feeling so lost, so full of regret, it was over. I felt only relief. And incredible gratitude. My parents loved me. My baby and I were saved.

Jack came along as Paul drove me to Southampton in his father's vintage Riley. It was a magnificent car, the one his father had carried me to our wedding ceremony in only four months before. In less than an hour we were at the ship's dock.

I couldn't wait to be gone. I don't even remember our goodbyes. I simply felt so grateful to be leaving Jack for the last time. I didn't even feel like crying over what a mistake those years had been; I was just thrilled to be safe and to know I could create a new life. I was young, I was happy. And I was going to have my baby I'd dreamed of for so long.

My morning sickness was gone after the first day of that five-day crossing. I was able to enjoy food again and everything was delicious. I was so hungry.

I made new friends, Peter and Heidi, newlyweds from Germany, who were on their honeymoon. I played bridge with some older women who thought I was adorable and brave, traveling alone, being pregnant and all. It was beautiful August weather, such an amazing contrast from that rough January crossing on the enormous Queen Elizabeth. Sailing on this much smaller ship on calm summer seas was smoother than a highway ride all the way to New York.

When we docked in New York and I got through customs, I took a taxi to La Guardia and after paying for my plane ticket, I arrived in Indiana two hours later with five dollars in my pocket.

TEN
LUCKING OUT: A NEW AND HAPPY LIFE
1963-1965

I was so nervous on the flight to Indianapolis, wondering what my parents were feeling. Would they be happy to see me? Would they be glad about my baby? Or would they feel ashamed of me? They didn't even know whether I had married or would soon become an unwed mother, adding to all the other shameful things I had done. I couldn't explain anything in the cable I'd sent, only that I was pregnant and needed money to come home.

During those three long weeks before they responded, I felt they must be done with me. And even when the wired cheque arrived, there was no message that came with it, so I had no idea whether they would forgive me for all the hurt I had caused them.

Back in those days, people who were waiting for loved ones

who were flying in, were allowed to stand outside on the tarmac, watching for passengers to walk down the stairs descending from the plane. This was years before there were jet bridges and people could walk off the plane and directly into the terminal.

As we landed and taxied closer, I saw my parents standing there on the tarmac, looking up expectantly at the airplane windows. They looked so small. The instant I saw them, my love for them both washed over me and I sobbed and I waved and I hoped they could see me. I could hardly wait to get off the plane and run to hug them.

They *were* happy to see me, but they were more reserved. My father, especially, looked older and tired. They didn't ask any questions on the drive home, just letting me talk. I told them how grateful I was for their help and how sorry I was about needing to ask them to rescue me. I said I knew I would be able to get a job right away and pay them back and handle my own expenses going forward. I hoped that they would be proud of me for leaving Jack. I told them I was sure I would become a mature, level-headed young woman. *Becoming a mother would make it so.*

We settled in together, and there was no criticism this time. My mother implored me not to talk about what had happened in St. Louis, or in England, or ever to mention Jack. "Can we just be happy now?" she pleaded. I assured her I was through with Jack forever. I had broken his spell at last.

The job that had eluded me in Southampton was waiting for me in Indianapolis. I was once again a working fashion artist. I had a wonderful art director, a lovely older woman who empathized with my situation of being pregnant and on the verge of divorce. Though we had little time for personal conversation, just her proximity there during my workday was comforting. I had been concerned about my work not really showing a personal style, but she convinced me that it did. She pointed out certain flourishes I had already developed and assured me that my style would continue to evolve during my career.

I loved working again, even though it was tiring in the last half of my pregnancy. Of course I wore high heels to work, because we all did, back in the day. There weren't any comfortable stylish shoes then. I would come home from work on the bus, walking half a block in those high heels to their home, where my mother would soon have dinner ready. While we waited for a casserole to finish baking, we would sit together on the couch, and while I told her the news of my day, she would rub my tired feet. This was such a loving gesture, and I was beginning to feel more relaxed with her, though my guard was never completely down. My father, though, was quieter than ever. He seemed to be pulling away from me, taking with him the love that I had always known.

Finally, on a cold and snowy January morning, my longed-for baby arrived. I was overjoyed when the doctor woke me, whispering in my ear. "She's a healthy, beautiful girl with blue eyes like yours," he said. The moment they put her in my arms, I knew her name. It was Jennifer, but I have always called her Jenny.

A child of my own to love and care for, and for the rest of my life. My heart was soaring. Thank God I have a girl, I thought, because I knew nothing about boys; not about sports, or fishing, or whatever else little boys might enjoy. But I'll know how to be a good Mommy for a girl. I was certain.

The last night before we were released from the hospital, I began to think of a timeline for our wonderful life together. By the time Jenny is 6 and begins school, I'll be 30. By the time she finishes school and goes to college, I'll be 43. As I was imagining all of this, thinking of a parade of life experiences we'd share, I stayed awake up until this one: when she turns 60, I'll be 84. And then I fell asleep.

By the time Jenny was born, I had repaid my parents the money they had cabled me in England and paid for my prenatal care and delivery: $365, plus all the hospital expenses. I had no insurance, but I was able to pay for the private room, $19.50 a day for three days. My mother and I were surprised that it seemed about the same cost as a good hotel room.

My parents loved Jenny and enjoyed her so much, they didn't want us to move to an apartment of our own, so for nearly two years we lived with them, and I paid them room and board. My job was downtown at one of the nice department stores, and I hired a woman to take care of my daughter during the afternoons, so my mother could continue to enjoy her part-time job, greeting newcomers to town.

In those wonderful early years, Jenny and I adored each other. We had such good times together. I told myself: *See, you were right. You can do this. It's just like you were sure it would be!*

When she was barely walking, I taught her how to read with flash cards. At bedtime every night she wanted me to read her the story of *Goodnight Moon*. When she looked out the window and saw the clouds in the night sky beginning to cover the moon, she would always remind me, "The clouds are the Moon's blankies."

One afternoon, when she was 22 months old, I was slowly brushing the back of her long fine hair, and we had both become still. Then suddenly, but quietly and even matter-of-factly she said, "I remember being born."

What? I was shocked and so excited! I had read in a pregnancy booklet before leaving England that sometimes little children will say they remember being born. They might say "it was dark" or "I was cold". Of course, in my excitement, I wanted to turn her around to see her face, yet I knew I couldn't interrupt this moment, or it would pass.

Trying to be calm and sound conversational, I continued brushing her hair.

"What was it like?" I asked.

"We were standing in line, behind God," she answered, "waiting for our turn."

All in one sentence. Matter-of-factly. And even though this sounded like her voice, it was way beyond her speech pattern at that age.

Phenomenal. I was stunned. I felt so privileged to hear this astonishing recall of such a miraculous event, her own birth! Most extraordinary of all, she recalled the Other Side. *She remembered being with God.* Desperately wanting to know more, I tried gently to coax it from her, but she said nothing else. I continued brushing her hair, hoping that this was what was putting her in a reverie, something that many years later I would call an altered state of consciousness. But the veil between worlds had dropped.

When she spoke again it was to ask for a cookie, and she sounded like her normal, not quite 2-year-old self again. I sat there in awe. Breathless. I had to find out how a memory like this could be possible. I knew then that there must be so much more to discover, and I was determined to find it. It was the moment that began my search for what I would later begin calling the Mysteries.

When Jenny was two years old, I enrolled her at Ten Little Indians nursery school. I was so happy to see that she loved it immediately. How I adored watching the pure joy pouring out of her when I picked her up every evening after work. She would always ask:

"Can I go again tomorrow?" When I would answer "Yes!!" she would squeal with happiness. And we laughed and laughed at the wonder of such fun.

I would give anything to live those early days again. When all good things to come seemed inevitable.

Later, when Jenny was 3 years old, she was leafing through a scrapbook my mother had made of snapshots from my childhood. Looking at one particularly tiny photo-booth picture of me at age 7, she said it made her sad. She told me that she knew we had been friends when I was that age, but that she had later died. How did she even know about death?

I marveled then and I still do now at those revealing moments of her awareness of a past life together. Was there really such a thing as reincarnation? Could people actually experience other levels of consciousness? Hearing these memories from a child so young was such a miraculous gift to me. There was so much more I wanted to learn. But that was long before the internet. I didn't have any idea of how or where to find information like this.

I simply knew that I was being led to find those answers, and more.

Eleven

Trying Out: New York!
Testing my talent 1965

Life continued to be peaceful, joy-filled, calm. Until I told my parents that I wanted to find an apartment for Jenny and me to live on our own. My father said little. He dearly loved Jenny, but no longer seemed to pay much attention to me. I missed his affection, but I was so glad that he enjoyed my darling girl. My mother was very upset at the thought of a move. I tried to reassure her, saying "We'll still be right here in town. It's not like we're moving across the country like a lot of other young people do!"

I found a decent small apartment for us, only minutes away from their home, but I know it was a sad day for her. Still, I loved being on my own, able to provide for us both with my new job as an illustrator, now at the nicest store in town, and I was delighted to have Jenny in the nursery school she was loving so much.

Before her first birthday, I flew to St. Louis to divorce her father. I wore my blue wool suit which had last been worn when I was marrying Jack, wondering how long it would be before I would be standing here, divorcing him. He was ordered to pay me $50 a month for child support, but he never sent it.

Being on my own and feeling empowered revived my old dreams from all those movies of going to New York and searching for dazzling success. The security and comfort I had now acquired were no match for the longing I continued to feel for the excitement of new experiences. How else could I explain that even though I had such immense gratitude for my parents helping me, pregnant with Jenny, escape from my hapless adventure with Jack, I just had to leave. Was this the folly of youth, or was I simply being selfish?

From this vantage point, I can see that, yes, I was being selfish. This time I *was* going to move us "all across the country like a lot of other young people do" and I didn't really care whether my parents approved or not. I was incapable then of understanding how our absence would affect them. Even worse, I hadn't imagined how this move would affect Jenny.

To add to all that, I was full of "magical thinking." I may have been a professional as an artist, but I was an amateur at developing any foresight about the possible consequences of my life choices, for all of us, not for Jenny, not for my parents, not for myself.

Sherle Stevens

By the time I was 26, I was well enough known as a fashion illustrator in Indianapolis that I had been hired away from one department store to another, until I had worked for them all. Since I had collected the "tear sheets" from the newspapers from stores all over the country, in comparing my work to other artists, I finally felt that I was ready for the Big Time. I got my portfolio of sketches together, and, dressed in a smart new suit in my best Jackie Kennedy style, complete with hat and gloves, off I went to New York to try to prove it. It was 1965.

Most of the fashion illustrators were working freelance in New York, I found, and when I was making the rounds of the few department stores that hired fashion artists, there currently weren't any openings. I was surprised to see that their individual artist's offices were not as spacious and private as mine had been in all the stores in Indianapolis, where I had pinned photos on the walls of my cubicle and could listen to jazz on my radio all morning and afternoon while I drew and painted. I'd been able to move around the office at will and drop in on the cubicles of the other artists, seeing what they were up to. We were all office friends who celebrated each other's birthdays and applauded each other's good news. At the best store of all, where I was working currently, I was famous for routinely taking two hours for lunch, indulged by Gilbert, my wonderful art director who enjoyed me and loved my work.

But here in New York in the advertising offices at JC Penney, high up in their own impressive skyscraper, the artists were all in one enormous room, lined up in two long rows with their drawing boards touching the backs of the chairs of the artist sitting directly ahead. There must have been thirty of them.

When I arrived at my appointment, the receptionist pointed me toward a drawing board halfway down the first row where I found the woman who would interview me. She had no private office; I merely stood next to her while she went through my portfolio of sketches. Finally, she looked up to tell me they only hired layout artists, not illustrators. Even if she'd offered me a job, I couldn't bear to think of working there.

Through an employment agency I had an interview in a real office at McCall's Pattern Company, in that very tall iconic building at the end of Park Avenue. This seemed like a perfect place. And they hired me on the spot to illustrate the pattern covers. Finally, I was going to be a professional artist, living in New York, a real New Yorker, at last!

The next day I found a well-known artist's agent who took me on to represent me as part of her stable, which meant I could earn extra freelance income too. I felt so proud to have my work endorsed in New York, which has always been the proving ground for all creative work that interested me in art, drama, music, theatre, fashion - and of course, advertising.

I went back home feeling triumphant, excited to tell my parents about my success, expecting them to be proud of me, and happy for me too. They must have been terribly disappointed to think of losing Jenny and frightened too for us both. But once again, as on the night before I'd left for Europe, they said nothing, and once again, I was too absorbed in my own excitement to feel their pain. I began making plans for the Big Move.

I had just three weeks to find an apartment and a nursery school for Jenny before the day I would begin my wonderful new job. A friend was planning a trip to New York, and she agreed to bring Jenny with her on the plane as soon as I had everything in place.

So once again, off I went on my own, my technicolor visions in tow about how *my* New York story would unfold.

Twelve
Still Trying: Paul, School, First Day at McCalls 1965

Before I left Indiana, I'd had a letter from that darling, Paul Johnson, the kindest (and handsomest) friend, the one who had first sailed with Jack from Oslo, who had helped us cross the English Channel, then soon had been the Best Man at our wedding.

Dear Paul, who had brought me the art supplies when I tried to paint fashion samples sitting on the floor of the boat. Kind Paul, who had kept me going with fresh strawberries and soda crackers when that was all I could keep down in those first months of my pregnancy. Helpful Paul, who drove me in his father's car to Southampton to board the ship that helped me escape from Jack forever.

During the three years I'd been back in the States, Paul had made news, having sailed from England alone across the Atlantic Ocean on *Venus,* his own 13-foot Colin Archer, his decked-over Norwegian lifeboat. Since then, he had been living on his boat in Martinique and had written me that he was going to be in New York for an appearance on the *Today* show, so he would be sure to see me when I arrived.

And there he was, as soon as I got off the plane. Incredible to see him standing there and wearing a suit in civilization. And as handsome as ever, with his sea blue eyes, and his unruly curly black hair and beard.

We spent those three weeks together before Jenny arrived. For the first few nights until I found a place to live, he took me to stay with him at an enormous and elegant apartment right off Fifth Avenue in the East 80s that someone had offered him while he was in the city. There were other seemingly transient but professionally dressed young women and men, all temporarily bunking there as well. It seemed a little weird, but thanks. We had our own room, and it meant we didn't have to spend money on a hotel while I looked for an apartment for Jenny and me.

I had hunted in the newspaper want ads for apartments for rent in Indianapolis, but New York was having a newspaper strike. So I had to choose a neighborhood and just go up and down the streets searching for "For Rent" signs and checking out the apartments when I was able to find someone on the property to let me in. There were phone numbers on the signs, but this was 1965, light-years before mobile phones, and since I didn't already have an apartment, I didn't have a landline either.

After a few tiring days pounding the sidewalks on the Upper West Side, a neighborhood a college friend had recommended, I found something in my price range, $150 @ month. It was on West 76th between Broadway and West End Ave. Undoubtedly a more upscale area today, but at the time it was nicknamed "Needle Park" because of the proliferation of drug addicts, so you can imagine.

I found a blue Danish couch left out on the street for anyone to take, as people do in the city. Paul, with the help of a couple of guys walking by, managed to get it up the steps into the building on to the elevator, and down the hall to my new apartment. My agent gave me a bed that Jenny and I could share. I found a few necessary items at Macy's including a lamp with a white glass globe which became the only light in the place except for the overheads in the bathroom and bedroom and over the sink in the tiny kitchenette that was closed off by a folding leatherette partition. The bathroom had no windows, and every feature, the sink, the toilet, the painted walls and the tub, was a slightly varied shade of Pepto-pink. I always felt a little nauseous in there.

One evening as I sat in the suds in my bright pink bath, I heard music and people talking as loudly as if they were in the tiny room with me. What on Earth? I looked up and saw a vent above the shower head and figured that had to be the source of the noise. When I'd finished bathing and let the water drain out, I dressed quickly, grabbed a small table and was able to place it so I could stand up and see if the vent was open. Was it ever! I looked right into a tiny kitchen only inches from my nose where a man and a woman were cooking their dinner. There was no way to close the vent, so I knew then not to ever sing in the shower which might invite my neighbors to get on a chair and peep in. In my tiny living room, the walls were so thin that I could have carried on a conversation with the people next door. But it was New York, and now I lived here! It was heaven.

We became lovers from that first night. Adorable Paul, who had lived his entire life on ocean-going boats, sometimes moored, and often sailing the seas all over the Atlantic and Pacific Oceans, invited me (and Jenny, who was soon due to arrive) to leave with him as he was itching to return to Martinique. Such a dear man, and what a magnificent lover! But leave New York, my life's dream? There was no way. I had a fabulous job waiting! And I couldn't even imagine taking my tiny girl to live that lifestyle we had just escaped.

Another time I might have made a different choice, because one thing I knew, even then: Paul was a good man, a kind person. I adored him. He was wonderful in every way, except that he lived on a boat.

Kindness is what I always look for in a friend but I had never yet found this dearest of qualities in a man. I was still so young and naive, and Jack's talents and adventurous nature had blinded me to his lack of that all-important ethic. I would only much later admit that it is the most important virtue to me.

Paul and I were both 27 years old then. As I was writing this, wondering if he was still alive, I began searching online for him. I found that he had become a legendary designer and builder of ocean-going boats; that later he had 3 wives, at different times, and had fathered a child with each of them. He had sailed and lived on his various boats all over the world and was beloved by other sailors everywhere. Well, no wonder. He was extraordinary in every way.

Sadly, I found that he had died not long ago at 82, only two years after a young woman director and crew from Slovakia met him in the Caribbean and were excited to make a documentary film about him, The Sailor, *which in 2021 won awards at seven international film festivals. I found that it was available on YouTube when I searched "The Sailor documentary."*

My heart flew wide open, just to see him again, looking at the film of him alive, along with so many still photos of him at the various ages he eventually became. What a gift this film is for all of us who once knew and loved this beautiful man; what a testament to Paul's extraordinary spirit. I'm sure he was especially delighted that it was a beautiful young woman who had last found him fascinating and wanted to capture his amazing story.

Paul had sailed away, and now my darling Jenny was arriving! I took a taxi to the airport to greet her and my friend Melda, her chaperone. I was so happy to lift her into my arms again! I had thought the plane ride would have been great fun for her, but she seemed subdued. Melda told me that she had expected to find me on the plane and was disappointed.

When we arrived back at the apartment, as soon as she walked in, before even letting me take off her coat, she said, "Your apartment is very nice," as she traced her fingers along a little table her size.

"Oh, Sweetheart!" I said, "It's not *my* apartment, it's *our* apartment! This is where we live now!"

We'd only been apart for three weeks, yet it seemed as if she thought I was someone she was visiting. I felt a catch in my heart. And prayed that it was just my imagination, and that being together again would quickly seem as wonderful as it had always been.

In those weeks before Jenny arrived, I had phoned over fifty preschools in the city to find one that had room for her. It was already September and all of them were full except one, the Bernby School on the far Upper West Side at 103rd St. in Harlem. With no other choice, I registered her there and had to trust that everything would be fine.

Jenny had loved her Ten Little Indians school so much, and I prayed that she would love it here too. I knew she was accustomed to me leaving her to go to work and picking her up at the end of the day. It had never been a problem for her to see me go; she loved school.

When she was ready for her first day at Bernby, I realized I couldn't bear to think of taking her on the subway. So we left early, and I carried her across Broadway to catch an uptown bus on the other side of the street. On the first day the school's owner met me in the lobby of an old office building. I hugged Jenny goodbye and told her I would see her after work. I wasn't invited to see the school itself, which I assumed was somewhere in the building. But I told myself it would be fine.

I raced down several blocks to catch the subway at an express stop that would take me all the way down to Times Square, where I moved quickly through that enormous web of corridors to change to a crosstown train that would let me out on Park Avenue, praying that I would choose the proper corridor and get on the right train.

My first day at my wonderful new job, and my heart was racing in the elevator going up to the 42nd floor to the McCall's offices. I could hardly wait to see the setup and meet the other artists. I was sure it would be sophisticated and elegant, and my coworkers would be savvy and fun to know. The people who'd interviewed me had shown me nothing. And no wonder.

My expectations were shattered the instant I was brought to the room where I would be shown my place. The other two artists were working. Both looked up at me without smiling, only briefly acknowledging my presence.

One tiny woman seemed very old, probably three times my age. She did pause her work long enough to tell me that she'd been there twenty years, which is why she was allowed to sit next to the only window in the room. She seemed protective of her location, so I didn't walk close enough to see if she had a view of anything beyond a brick wall.

The other woman must have been only twice my age and was also seated next to the wall, just ahead of her. I don't think that either of them told me their names, or asked mine.

How I envied both their locations, since I was to be seated

behind a small drawing board in the middle of the room with space all around me, and only a tiny taboret table to hold my paints. To this day, I cannot bear to sit at tables in restaurants unless they are against a wall, or in a corner of the room. I'd rather be seated in a cozy booth.

As if the personal space issue weren't odd enough, since we didn't have any privacy with cubicles of our own, of course I couldn't play my little transistor radio. That would obviously be disturbing to the other two.

But then I was told we were not allowed to talk to each other. What? You're kidding, right? No wonder they hadn't been smiling at me; no reason to initiate a working friendship here.

So here I was, new in town, alone with a two-year-old child and hoping for some grownup conversation. Altogether this wasn't shaping up to resemble my dream at all. I also had a bad cold I'd picked up on the plane, that I couldn't seem to shake. Somewhere I'd read that a cold is unshed tears. *Hmmm.*

But by far the worst thing of all, was that each morning after that first day at Bernby School, Jenny would wrap her arms around my neck, sobbing and begging me not to leave her there. But I had no choice. She wasn't articulate enough at that age to tell me what was upsetting her. I had no idea. And I had to leave her there and go to work. Now both our hearts were breaking.

A week into clocking in at my drab new workplace, I had a call from my agent for a freelance job! The reference material was to be delivered to my apartment that evening and they wanted a finished painted sketch delivered by messenger by 9 a.m. the next morning. I was totally unprepared for this. Why had I wanted to sign up with an agent when I had a full-time job, anyway? I have no idea. It just seemed like the professional thing to do when I was on my job hunt, if I wanted to become a real New York artist.

I had read about this well-known agent in a trade publication that offered her phone number and address. I was so thankful that she granted me an interview and I was thrilled when she liked my portfolio and agreed to take me into her stable of artists.

When I returned to New York to begin my job, she invited me to dinner at her elegant apartment on the 16th floor in mid-Manhattan. I walked outside to the enormous balcony that extended beyond the wide expanse of windows in the dining room, where I could see all the way down to the Statue of Liberty. With a view from real estate like that, New York at night really does lie before you, dazzling like diamonds just like in the movies.

My eyes must have been huge and shining. Sylvia was caring and generous, noticing my sniffles and telling me I needed to take multi-vitamins. She gave me a large bottle of them. And when I told her I had to find a few pieces of furniture, she even had that bed delivered to my apartment.

Well, I couldn't disappoint her. Or risk losing an opportunity to land a free-lance job and earn some extra cash. Still, I was not set up to do the work. I had no drawing board and few art supplies.

I had no reference materials for poses, just like the time in England when I tried to create a portfolio to take to Southampton. I didn't even have a chair. So all night long I sat on the floor painting, like I had sat on the floor of the boat. And, without any sleep, I did a terrible job.

Bleary-eyed, I took the sketch with me to my office the next morning and called a messenger to pick it up. About 4:30 that afternoon, just before time to go home, where I intended to go to sleep right after dinner, my agent called me at work. The sketch was unacceptable to her client, she said, and they wanted me to re-do it overnight.

I have no idea how I lived through it, but after I put Jenny to bed, once again I was up all night, in tears, drawing and painting till dawn. This piece was even more awful than the first one. I was so embarrassed to send it, but off it went with the messenger. Naturally it was rejected. Which was the end of any more possibly lucrative free-lance work and any more contact with my famous agent.

I was so humiliated. What a life lesson. Obviously, I had to see that there was no way I could work a full-time job and be a free-lance artist. But that night, I was just utterly exhausted and simply grateful to be allowed to sleep. And, thankfully, I got to keep the bed.

Thirteen
FREAKING OUT: Blackout
November 9, 1965

Once again: Should I go or should I stay?

When I used to hear people bring out that old saw: "New York's a great place to visit, but I wouldn't want to live there," I would always say, "Well, I would!"

My love for all those movie musicals had convinced me that New York and I were a perfect match. I had been on my own with good jobs for six years by then and I had so much confidence in my ability, in my talent, in my determination. The fact that New York was bigger than the cities I'd been living and working in never gave me pause. I was certain that I was up to this town.

I'd been here for over two months now, and Jenny had been in school for several weeks when she came down with chicken pox, which became a ticket out of Bernby School for two weeks. It turned out to be an enormous gift from the Universe.

At the school's recommendation that to be safe, I should only work with an agency - I hired a bonded babysitter. A lovely woman came to stay with Jenny while I went to work. Since the two of them were there at the apartment waiting for me on November 9, 1965, I was able to take the subway straight home to our apartment on West 76th Street, instead of riding all the way up to 103rd St. to the Bernby School.

Even before she got sick, I knew Jenny was unhappy there, though she didn't ever tell me why. I felt terrible for her, knowing she had loved Ten Little Indians so much. But I had no choice: there was no other nursery school opening available. And here I was, leaving her every day to go to a job I had to admit that I didn't really like, either.

New York was hard to get used to living in day by day, starting with the morning race uptown with Jenny on the bus, then dashing several blocks to the express station and standing all the way in the rush hour subway ride, being crammed in so tight and felt up by men on all sides. At least I thought they were men. I didn't look. I always wore sunglasses and kept my eyes down. I was grateful that it was cold enough to wear my buttoned-up long suede coat so they couldn't get far. The crime rate was high, and I'd heard that people were frequently stabbed in the subway cars. So it was a relief to have a shorter ride that night.

Feeling so sad for Jenny and disillusioned with my job and honestly, with living in New York, I had been downcast for days. But this evening, walking the few blocks up Broadway from the subway station, I suddenly brightened. Here I had been in my old familiar quandary for days: should I go? Or should I stay? But now I had a funny feeling that something significant would happen that very night that would help me know which road to take. I thought it might be a letter or a phone call from someone back home.

I turned the corner from Broadway onto West 76th, walked past two buildings and into my own. I took the elevator to the 10th floor, got out, walked down the hall to my apartment, put my key in the door, and walked in just as the light bulb in that globe lamp I'd bought at Macy's, the only light in the living room, slowly darkened as if it were on a dimmer switch.

It was already very dark outside at 5:30 p.m. At first, I was just upset that now I'd have to spend money on a new light bulb, that's how tight my budget was. Then, as I was pressing my face against my one small window, where I could always see a sliver's width of streetlights and lights from the stores along Broadway, tonight there were no lights at all. Wow, it was affecting more than my lamp, or our building. It was the whole neighborhood!

My phone rang and it was the agency calling for the babysitter. I handed her the phone. Something much bigger than a letter or a phone call was happening to change my life, and the lives of 30 million others. This was no neighborhood problem, this was a total blackout that covered 80,000 square miles!

The agency told her to ask me if she could spend the night with us since it was pitch black out and there was no way for her to get home. Of course! I was grateful for the company. It was wonderful to have a grownup New Yorker to talk to and to question.

I began shaking at the thought that I had so narrowly escaped being stranded in the subway. I learned later that more than 800,000 riders were trapped in New York City's subways that night with the trains stopped in total darkness, and with no idea why. Eventually police rescued them with flashlights, and they all had to climb out of the trains and step over several rails. I heard that they had to be especially careful not to touch their feet on the third rail, which could electrocute them if the power was suddenly switched back on.

I had also just missed being trapped in the elevator that I had been in only five minutes before. But the most miraculous gift of all, if not for the chicken pox, Jenny would have been waiting for me at school and I wouldn't have come. I was shaking even more, thinking of how frightened she would have been, and how frantic I'd have been, unable to reach her. I was incredibly grateful we were home safely together.

I had no television set, but I turned on my tiny transistor radio and heard Walter Cronkite's voice, and it was shaking. Dear God! His voice hadn't been shaking when he announced the terrible assassination of President John Kennedy just two years earlier. Now he was telling us that the whole Eastern Seaboard was blacked out and that it wasn't possible for this to have been an accident; there were too many fail-safe operations in place for that to happen.

"We have no idea what this is. It could be the Russians!"

His voice shook even more. This was during the height of the current Cold War.

I stayed awake for hours listening to the babysitter's stories. She told me about many of her experiences babysitting for people at different income levels, some of them even famous, including a man who was currently the star of a major musical on Broadway. "This is not a wonderful place to raise children," she said. "The poor ones aren't the only ones who suffer. The wealthy children all have their own therapists and parents who are hardly ever home." Funny. Until now, I had thought it would be such a wonderful place to raise children, with the best symphonies, theatres, libraries, museums and a hundred other splendors to investigate.

But her stories showed me a different side entirely. And I could see that with my work wearing me down daily, there wasn't much of me left over for Jenny in the evenings or on weekends. No grandparents to visit here, either. How selfish and short-sighted I had been, thinking only of my dreams and expecting everything would be happy for her, just because I loved her so much. But Bernby School wasn't Ten Little Indians.

When I woke the next morning, even before I left for work, I knew the answer to "Should I stay? Or should I go?" Even without the chocolate.

Fourteen
Leaving Out: A Big Detail, Blizzard, Taxi, Gone 1965

I begged the airline agent when I made the reservation over the phone- "I only have enough money for one ticket. I have to leave New York and go home to Indiana. Would you let me hold my 2-year-old daughter on my lap?" Thank God, she said yes.

Three months after I moved in, and after giving McCall's two weeks' notice, we took French Leave of the apartment, walking out without giving the management notice, leaving everything behind: the blue Danish couch, the agent's bed, the globe lamp from Macy's, even wastebaskets unemptied. It was the only possible way. I felt guilty even as I tried to assure myself that it must happen every day in this town where young people from less sophisticated parts of the country swarm here, hoping to make it, and then for one reason or another, give up on their dreams. Stephen Sondheim's song "Another Hundred People" from the musical *Company* tells the story stingingly.

The morning of our flight it was snowing. By the time we got down to the lobby it was turning into a blizzard. The wind was incredibly strong. I was hurting so much; I didn't even stop to wonder if the planes were flying. I was just desperate to get a taxi. I knew they wouldn't be coming down our side street, that to have a hope of finding one, I would have to make it down to Broadway, which was close, or far down to West End Avenue in the other direction.

My dear little Jenny looked so tiny, standing there beside our suitcases, her sweet face visible through the glass door of the lobby, watching me walk away from her. I could hardly bear the sorrow and the guilt I felt for what I had dragged her into: this ruined dream of mine, coming here to New York, away from her grandparents and the nursery school she loved...for what?

When I finally hailed a taxi, we had to go all the way around the long blocks because of one-way streets in a slow-motion ride that felt like hours as the snow blew hard and piled higher. We arrived at last to fetch my sweet girl who had patiently stood right where I'd left her. I gathered her and our suitcases, and we began that frightening ride through more blowing snow than I'd ever seen.

I didn't even watch the blizzard through the taxi's windows to see if we were going to be able to make it to the airport; I only wanted to hold Jenny and tell her everything was going to be all right.

"We're going home to Nana and Bampa! You'll get to go back to Ten Little Indians with Bob and Marla again!"

But that didn't seem to matter to her. She looked at me.

"What's a Daddy? Do I have one?"

And my heart cracked open and flew into pieces – flying around like that blinding snow. This was the first time she had noticed that some of the other children had Daddies instead of Mommies picking them up from school.

I tried hard to swallow my pain and prayed to sound upbeat.

"Oh yes, of course you have one! Your Daddy's name is Jack and he lives in California, and someday we'll go see him!" I hope I told her that he loved her very much. And oh, how I wished that were true.

Finally, miraculously, we arrived at La Guardia and the planes were flying. She was allowed to travel sitting on my lap as the agent had promised, and before long we were returned once more to my parents' loving and forgiving arms. I was deeply thankful.

On Monday, Bob and Marla and the littles at Ten Little Indians were so happy to see Jenny return. Though we'd only been away for three months on this doomed adventure, to me it seemed like a year or more. I had so much to learn about life. I kept finding out the hard way that it is not like the movies.

Darling Gilbert gave me my old job back. We moved into a new apartment and got a dog.

In a few months Jenny turned three and began taking ballet lessons.

Life moved on for us both. I licked my wounds. I let go of my now horribly tarnished dream of living in New York. I thought Jenny and I were both healing and moving on. Life began to seem easy and fun again. And we were so close.

Fifteen
COMING OUT #1: CHRISTOPHER, TED 1965

My mother was creative in the way she decorated our home, in the way she dressed. I didn't know if she might have longed for a creative career; she'd never said. But that wouldn't have been a likely ambition for her to hope for, growing up in the 1920's.

It wasn't till after my father died, six years after I returned from this job with McCall's Patterns in New York, that my mother told me that she had been offered a job with Advance Patterns in New York when I was about 12 years old.

"Don't you remember when we went to Chicago and bought all those dresses for you?" she said.

"When we got home, I took your picture wearing each one. I'd been corresponding with several pattern companies, telling them there were no appropriate dresses in the stores for girls your age when you were 11. Everything was either too childish or too sophisticated. Advance Pattern Co. sent me a check for $50 to buy you dresses and we drove to Chicago to try to find the best. When I sent them the pictures and they saw what I had chosen, they offered me a job as a dress designer."

I was astounded! How had she kept this to herself all these years?

"How fabulous! Why didn't you take it?" I said.

"Your father could never have found a job in New York," she answered.

That would have been far more prestigious than the job I had just left. What must it have been like for her to watch me go to New York and find work? And at a pattern company!

My heart hurt for her. Imagine feeling that she had to turn down an incredible offer like that, to be dress designer! It must have been devastating to her. And then, to keep it a secret, to not even be able to share the joy of having been chosen. Her one and only big chance.

What a gift I was given to be able to come back to the job I had left when I went to New York. What a contrast to that dreary room at McCall's Pattern Company; the office may have been located on posh Park Avenue, but my four square feet of it was hell.

And now here I was, back in my dear little cubicle, the one with the cork-covered walls I could pin my favorite photos on, and the sideboard where I could spread out all my paints and charcoal crayons and set my transistor radio so I could once again listen to jazz all day long while I sketched and painted. How great I felt. I was again the head fashion artist for the best store in town, and I was only 26. My darling art director Gilbert was thrilled to take me back, and even gave me a raise.

Once again, I could get up from working at my drawing board and walk around to chat with my co-workers whenever I wanted. This privilege I had always taken for granted and, oh, how I'd missed it.

I was back in town with old friends, too. Of course, it was Indianapolis, not the exciting city New York will always be for me. But with a two-year-old child to care for, and a full-time job, I hadn't been able to enjoy the places I loved about the city. I didn't have the time to go to museums or the money to go to restaurants, nightclubs, or Broadway shows. I was unable to drink in all the creative excitement that drew me to New York in the first place.

I didn't even have a way to meet any young men who would take me to those places. That dreary setup at McCall's might as well have been the local advertising office at a Woolworth's 5 & 10 Cent Store, Anywhere, USA. Outside of the two women in my room, I never saw another employee beyond the two bosses I reported to. They would both have to okay my sketches with their initials before I was allowed to render the finished paintings of the designs that would be featured on the pattern covers. Dull. Dull. Dull. And dreary.

Now that I was back home, I had my parents who loved to take care of Jenny when I wanted to go out with friends. In other words, I had a life again. And since they were so happy to have Jenny back, they were glad to see me too, without lecturing me on how foolhardy I'd been to go to New York in the first place. All was well.

How alive I felt...in addition to my thirst for adventure, I was so full of still untapped sexual longing. I fell in love many times. Even with gay men who loved me back, but not that way.

There was Christopher. Beautiful. Talented. Haunted by memories of his father mocking him and calling him Miss Hampton. He played concert level piano; listening to his Chopin made me cry. With charcoal crayons, he made languid fashion sketches. What I loved most was that he got me.

Four years younger and just out of a California art school, Chris was my friend the moment Gilbert hired him not long before I left for New York. I was so happy to see him at his drawing board when I returned.

Chris and I adored each other. We would dash over to a hotel near the store for lunch in a dark bar, eating, laughing, drinking whiskey sours and talking about all the plans we had for ourselves.

He was just then in the process of coming out to himself, finally admitting that he was gay. It was painfully inconvenient since he was engaged to be married to a girl he had dated in high school. In fact, her engagement photo was scheduled to appear that coming Sunday on the prestigious front page of the women's section of the city's largest newspaper.

"Chris, you've got to tell her!" I said, "You've got to stop this *now*, before it goes any further!"

He was terrified to end it. The wedding invitations had already been mailed. His mother would have to face the women at the Happy Mother's Club in shame.

"But you can't let that minor embarrassment make you go through with this," I said. "You can't ruin this poor girl's life, and *yours*, not to mention the lives of any children you might have!"

He finally agreed that the future fallout would be worse than the whipping he would take in the now. It was probably the best thing I ever did for someone I had never even met, this innocent young woman, Susie. And certainly, for Chris as well.

He limped through the emotional beating from both the families and told me he was forever grateful for my coaching.

But he couldn't seem to be happy being gay either. This was still 1965, four years before the Stonewall Riots in New York brought national attention to the fight for equal rights for LGBTQ people. And we were in the ultra-conservative Midwest. It was not safe for him to be out.

Of course, once Susie was dispensed with, I had Chris all to myself, emotionally at least. And of course, needy and unfulfilled, fresh from my divorce and the pain of losing my New York dream, I easily fell in love with this beautiful, creative soul who knew me so deeply and loved me too. We had our own "in" jokes. He said when we were old, we should get an Airstream trailer and paint on the back "2 TIRED 2 DRAW 4 U". It was such fun as we dreamed of who we could become in the meantime.

But before long, after the fiasco of ending his engagement and the fallout with his family, he felt he needed to get away from Indianapolis. He headed out, intending to return to L.A., where he had felt free to be himself during the years he was in art school.

On his way out West, he stopped in Dallas to have an interview at Neiman Marcus where they gave him a fabulous job offer. He decided to take it and soon began therapy, telling me he hoped he could recover from being gay so we could be a real couple together. I knew nothing about the possibility of that; I just hoped he would find the inner peace he seemed never to have known. I knew he loved me, and I felt that even if he remained gay, we would always love each other as friends.

Then one night he called me, crying and saying that he had just returned from a therapy session and that he realized he would always be gay. I was expecting it, really, and I tried to be strong and supportive. But I was not expecting his next words; he could never see or even speak with me again. I was sickened. I begged him.

"Please don't say goodbye forever!" But he said, "I just have to!" and hung up.

I called a girlfriend to come spend the night with me. I was afraid to face such pain alone. She listened patiently to me sobbing out my story and then encouraged me to try to get some sleep, promising to be there all night.

The next morning, I called work to tell Gilbert, who totally understood, probably more than I did. Years later, I learned he was gay too. He cared about me, wanting to help me get through this.

"Don't try to come in to work," he said. "Get out of this cold weather. Just get on a plane for Miami! It's Thanksgiving weekend, no one at the store will care, your work is all turned in. Get in the sun, have a change of scene and you'll feel better when you come back Monday."

Ted, the fascinating (and married) man who owned the engraving company that photographed our fashion drawings for the newspaper ads, had been flirting with me for weeks. He offered to drive me to the airport. I thanked him and flirted back all the way there. How desperately I was yearning for love and passion.

In the bar of my hotel, I met Sam and Charlie, two delightful men my age. Since they were interested in me, but without flirty sexual advances, they were probably gay too. And so much fun. We were all enjoying each other and when I told them the story of my recent heartbreak, they were determined to buoy me up.

We met on the beach the next day. When they learned I was an artist, they said, "Well, then we're off to find an art supply store!" They bought me a sketch pad and some charcoal crayons and then we returned back to the beach where we spent all afternoon drinking margaritas, while I sketched them. They were such dears, making me laugh and momentarily forget my sorrow. I told them about my ride to the airport.

"I think I'm probably going to go home and fall in love with a married man!" I said.

It was a fate I already knew I wanted, even though I'd never have believed I could sink to that level.

Sam and Charlie were leaving that next morning, so the following evening I went to another bar that had dancing with live music. A kind-looking young man asked me to dance. We sat at a table afterward sharing our stories. He had recently lost his fiancé, who had died suddenly. I told him about Chris. We were both so raw that we weren't capable of further conversation. We went out to his car. Not to make love or even to have mindless sex. We just held each other tight and sobbed without letup, to release at least some of the pain.

Sixteen
Sneaking Out: Falling For Ted 1965

When I returned from Miami, I did exactly as I'd told Sam and Charlie I would. I tossed aside what scruples I once had and began an affair with Ted.

He was friendly and gently flirtatious, and good-looking; he was a wealthy businessman nine years my senior. Ted was unlike any man I'd been attracted to yet in my young life. But then I hadn't been out in the world much yet, since my relationship with Jack had begun as a college romance.

I may sound cavalier now, but at the time I was not. Even as I felt guilty to let myself fall in love and lust with a married man, Ted was irresistible to me. We had such an extraordinary sexual chemistry that I willingly let myself be swept away.

Except for those romantic three weeks with Paul in New York, my previous intimate experience had been only with Jack.

In addition to his other faults, Jack had been a selfish lover, never interested in my pleasure, so I didn't have any.

Like Paul, Ted too was a romantic, very interested in our shared good times. And he treated me with admiration and respect. I felt loved, admired, desired. I was listened to and heard. This relationship was more than everything I'd wanted and never had.

He was very forthcoming in admitting that he'd had some affairs in the past because his marriage was unhappy for him, and for his wife too; they only stayed together to raise their two sons. But he made me feel that our romance was different from those other affairs, even as he told me, fairly enough, that he wouldn't divorce her because of the boys, whom he loved dearly.

He seemed so honest about his situation, telling me all of that because he said he would never want to hurt me. I knew where I stood, and I tried not to think of myself as being the another woman because everything else was so wonderful. My parents said little. They were just happy to have Jenny back in town and loved spending time with her. So I didn't feel I had to defend myself with them about Ted. By this time, I'm sure they had given up trying to influence my decisions.

At this juncture, I must tell you something I at first found ironic. I thought that arty-and-adventurous, fly-by-the-seat-of-his-pants, arrogant raconteur Jack couldn't be further removed from a man like Ted, the nice, friendly, worldly, upstanding family man, responsible company president, scion of a third-generation business. But here's what they actually had in common: They were both Marines in the Korean War. They both collected antique swords and flintlock pistols from the Revolutionary and Civil Wars. What's more, they both collected cannons; (Jack stole a cannon from the Isle of Wight after I left England, and had it shipped to me as a garden ornament so it would clear customs.) They both had Beagle dogs; Jack named his boat the *Cutlass*, and Ted, who owned a collection of 14 cars, most of them vintage sports cars, including an MG just like Jack's - preferred driving to work in his Pontiac, which he called by its model name, the *Cutlass*, as in "I'm taking the Cutlass to work today."

Weird? I thought so. Especially when their personalities seemed such a contrast, and the ways they treated me were as different as night and day. In my naivete, it took me a few years to discover what they shared that was the most significant for me.

Six months into our affair, Ted told me that he had fallen in love with me and that he was going to ask his wife for a divorce after all. I was in heaven, and he seemed elated too when he later told me that she had said, "Fine! But you're going to have to take these boys with you –I'm not raising them by myself!"

Ted said he felt like he'd hit the jackpot, getting everything he'd wanted.

But three weeks later, his wife was diagnosed with stage four cancer. Of course, he could not, certainly would not leave her now. So, for six years, until her death, we continued our affair, meeting each day for lunch. He would pick me up outside my department store office downtown. We would drive out to my apartment in the suburbs during the years Jenny was in nursery school, then later in grade school, for a stolen hour of passion.

Afterward we would pick up lunches to go and eat in the car on the way back downtown to our respective offices, laughing all the way. And of course, I still had my wonderful art director Gilbert, who continued to indulge my two-hour lunches.

Occasionally we would take a short trip, once even flying to Nassau for a long weekend, bringing Jenny along. Those were the good years. Ted and I were together every day during the week, he was home every night for dinner and 99% of the weekends. In all those years we were always on the same page. I could remember only one argument ever, and it was quickly healed. I immediately forgot what it was even about.

I felt grateful for such a long unbroken period of happiness, even if once again, I was living in sin and didn't yet have the sanctity of marriage. Still, I was fulfilled in ways I'd never known, so happy, and deeply in love. Life was good.

Until one Sunday afternoon when Jenny was five years old.

Before crossing a street in a quiet neighborhood after a birthday party, I reached back to take her hand. She yanked it away. I turned to look at her and saw an expression of terrible anger on her face. She was suddenly furious. "I liked it better when *I* was the Mother, and *you* were the Little Girl!" It was like a cord had snapped in two. Or a door had slammed shut.

Actually, it was all that and more.

It was the out-loud announcement of karma arriving. *It was the day I gave away my power to my child...*

And then, in the midst my happiness with Ted, and my new concerns with Jenny, came heartbreak; my sweet gentle father was diagnosed with end-stage cancer. And before long he passed away, but not without finally speaking directly to me. I was telling him how much I'd always loved him. He took my hand and said how much he'd always loved me, and that was what really mattered to him. The anguish of losing him felt unbearable; there was no point in living if this is how it ends, I thought.

In April, a year after my father's death, Ted's wife passed away.

One day shortly after her funeral, maybe a week or two later, he called me at work to ask me to meet him for lunch at a nice restaurant. This was odd. For all those years we'd had our lunchtime trysts virtually every weekday, our "nooners," those wonderful rolls in the hay. What could this be? Maybe an official proposal?

When I arrived at the restaurant, he looked serious, even a little nervous, an unfamiliar mood for Ted, who was always so cheery.

"You know, she's just died," he said, "and I think it would look so unseemly if we married right away."

I could certainly understand that. I could be patient a little longer. After all, I'd already waited six years. What was the harm in another month or two?

And then Ted went on, "I think I should date around a little first." *Huh??*

I had totally misunderstood this man I loved. Although my memory is quite sharp for most of the important moments in my life, I cannot recall exactly what I said. But here's the gist of it.

"Are you FUCKING KIDDING ME???"

Now I saw the setup: his expectation that I would not make a scene in a restaurant – that I would be forced to agree with him. But he was wrong. I raised my voice. And I told him that if he didn't marry me soon, I was done.

Wedding plans were made, and we married in early June at a stately Episcopal Church. Through what must have been gritted teeth, Ted's posh parents hosted a beautiful reception for us at their elegant estate, which of course included Jenny and my recently widowed mother, along with my aunts, uncles and cousins who'd flown in for the whole celebration. I don't believe there was a single friend of Ted's or his sons' or his parents' there. But I was too giddy to notice at the time. And Ted acted much happier to be getting married than Jack had been in England, so I thought we'd left behind all that "dating" talk, and that we were as much in love as we'd always been.

A week before our wedding, Ted told me that his wealthy parents had given him an enormous sum for a down payment on a large new home and he drove me there to see it. It was an elegant English Tudor, in an expensive neighborhood, and he said he'd already bought it. The house was so beautiful, and I loved it immediately. I was so naive, I thought he'd bought it without me along because he wanted to give me a wonderful surprise.

Well, the laugh was on me. Because they were probably sensing that this marriage wouldn't last, he said that his parents told him that he couldn't put my name on the deed. Come to think of it, in view of later arrangements Ted made with yet another upcoming wife, I'm sure that leaving me out of it had been his idea. I imagine he was already saving it for her. In fact, she may even have picked it out herself. But that's way ahead of my story...

SEVENTEEN
MOVING OUT - DIVORCE/ BETRAYAL 1973

In the beginning, we had a good time. Once again, I was happy to finally be legal and no longer living in sin, especially as the other woman. But with three children in the house, who bedrooms were right down the hall, our sex life disappeared. Even though Ted had told me of those other affairs before ours, I pushed that aside in my mind, assuring myself that he was different now because he really loved me and wouldn't be looking for more romantic adventures.

That was another of my incredibly naive ideas. To say that I was unprepared for life is such an understatement that it might be comic if it hadn't been so tragic, at least for me. He seemed to move around just fine.

I had asked Ted if he wanted me to continue working, and he told me it didn't matter to him, I could decide what I wanted to do. We didn't need two incomes, so I enjoyed staying home and taking painting classes, creating a studio on the enclosed sunporch where I painted portraits of my friends. If I'd been wise, I would have kept my job, expecting to continue meeting for our romantic lunchtimes, while the children were in school.

In October we went to a society Halloween party given at the local art museum. There were many different types of fortune-tellers giving readings and I was especially excited to see one I had heard about, a numerologist who had given a reading to a friend. He was very popular, and I had to wait in line. When it was my turn, I told him my name and birthdate, and what he said amazed me.

"You lost your father last year when you were 32." It was true! This was my first experience at having any sort of reading, and it was so exciting.

Next, I wanted to go to see the palm readers. Ted and I sat down next to each other at the table. A woman reached for my hand and the man next to her took Ted's. She saw something, but she seemed to be having misgivings about telling me. I heard the man telling Ted that he saw a baby. I wanted to have Ted's child and I was so happy to hear this. But when he saw my delight, Ted's reader signaled my reader to lean close to him. He began to whisper to her, and I knew they were seeing something they weren't going to say out loud. Were they seeing the baby in Ted's hand, but not in mine? They began to speak of other things to both of us. But I had an uneasy feeling I couldn't shake. Only later did I feel Ted beginning to pull away from me, but so slightly that at first, I didn't have to believe it.

It was quite a change for me at 33 to be stepmother to these two high school boys who had recently lost their mother. I was in *way* over my head, but I didn't know it. I had no older wiser women friends who might have been able to advise me as we began to face hurdles in this new family setup.

I had already met Terry, the older boy who was 17. Ted had introduced us several months before we were married. Terry wasn't close to his mother, and he began to stop by my apartment at times to ask my advice on his way home after dates. Sometimes he would bring his girlfriends to meet me, and we got along well.

It was 16-year-old Tim, who had been close to his mother, who became the problem. Obviously, he was in grief. But he was also on drugs, and Ted ignored it. Tim was high on quaaludes most of the time. I was very concerned that 9-year-old Jenny was coming into this environment. She was excited to meet her new brothers. She especially liked Tim.

Many years later, Ted told me that Tim walked unannounced into his office, after having been in India with the Peace Corps for the previous two years, and apologized.

"I'm sorry I ruined your marriage" he said.

As it turns out, the plot thickens, and it wasn't Tim's fault at all. He was merely the smoke screen for the real event that killed it.

Ted and his first wife did not hold compatible views on child-rearing (or so he told me) and evidently there had been many arguments about what the boys could and could not do. So, when we were first married, Ted told the boys that he and I were on the same page with how we wanted to raise them. He instituted family meetings and presented the two of us as a happy united front, where we adults would discuss our feelings about the latest exploits of the boys. The childish pranks, like putting cherry bombs in rural mailboxes were no longer to be tolerated, and there were to be *no* drugs: a *zero* tolerance policy. Nevertheless, Tim seemed to be zoned out every evening. Terry appeared to be fine. At least he didn't seem to be on anything.

One afternoon a policeman brought both boys home. They had been shoplifting stereo equipment. I was furious that they hadn't been arrested, but just brought home because our family (Ted's, not mine, of course, was wealthy.) When I asked Ted why he didn't let them go downtown to jail, he said, "You wouldn't let that happen to Jenny!"

"Oh yes, I would, if she'd done something illegal." I said. "I would want her to feel the effects of that immediately, hopefully as a major deterrent!"

I had asked him if we could please see a therapist for Tim, but even though Ted had a university degree in psychology, he was adamantly against it. The "what-would-people-think" worry. Evidently, Ted must have wanted that degree just so he could understand the psychology of getting his way in the business world. So there we were, becoming untethered, as if one of us was in a boat that was untied and floating out to sea. That one was me. Ted must have known exactly what he was doing.

One night during this tense time, Jenny came into our bedroom shortly after midnight to wake us, saying the house was filling with smoke. Because she was so much younger and had gone to bed much earlier, she woke and saved all our lives. We all ran outdoors in our pajamas and the firemen were there within minutes. They found that the furnace had been about to catch fire. I felt that this was the third time she saved my life; the first by being born, then by staying home with chicken pox in New York.

Family Meeting nights became less and less a showcase of parental unity. Months went by; we all stayed in our own worlds. I was driving Ted's snappy red Corvette to my portrait painting class at the Art Students League. The boys were going to school and doing whatever else they wanted to, and Jenny was in the 4th grade at a new school. Ted was busy running his company. Now that we were married, our passionate lunch hour trysts were a thing of the past. At least they were for me. I began to wonder if he was still having them with someone else. But I pushed those thoughts away.

Ted knew I wanted a child with him, but he said no. So I tried to just enjoy being a housewife for the first time, not having to worry about paying the bills myself. And having plenty of time to paint. We had our beautiful English Tudor house, a new home for all of us. We were all starting over. Or so I hoped.

After Christmas, Ted and I went on a delayed honeymoon to Europe. My mother came to stay to run the household for the two weeks we were gone. By the time we left for this trip, I could feel that our marriage, under this glare of real life, was becoming painful for both of us. I thought it was because of the boys that we were becoming distant. Ted stopped bothering with the Family Meetings.

Obviously, Tim was suffering and now Jenny was acting out. Her teacher called me to school and handed me a sexually suggestive note she'd confiscated that Jenny had passed to a boy in her 4th-grade class. At first I was shocked, but I could feel her energy shifting. Puberty was awakening. Maybe being in a house with these good-looking teenage boys was accelerating it.

There was something secretive about her now and we'd begun to lose the closeness we'd always shared. That must be a normal part of growing up, but I missed the sweetness between us. Aside from my parents, we had always had only each other. It was so different now, sharing life and our home with all this male energy. Once again, I was completely out of my element. Everything was changing.

One evening, not long after our return from Europe, a Family Meeting was suddenly called about Tim. I was so glad that Ted was paying attention to him at last, and I made a suggestion. Miles away from how he'd begun these meetings just months earlier, telling the boys that he and I were a united front, Ted turned and snapped at me.

"He's not *your* son!" he yelled. And I did something I've never done to anyone. I slapped his face.

In that instant, I was done. I told Jenny to get her schoolbooks. I threw some clothes for both of us in a bag and called my friend Carol who lived across the street to ask if we could please come over and spend the night.

"Yes, of course," she said.

My marriage ended on the spot.

Eighteen
Crying Out: Leaving Ted, Salt Lake City 1973-1975

I immediately regretted the slap and the screaming, and my impetuous flight across the street to Carol. I left in tears, hoping that somehow an intermediary could set up marriage counseling for us.

The next morning, I drove downtown to see Doug Sterns, a friend of Ted's who owned an ad agency. I'd known Doug during all those years of our affair, and I had thought he was happy for us.

I fully expected that he would be sympathetic, would see how much I was hurting, how much I loved Ted, and would reason with him to reconcile. I hoped that he might tell me that Ted was sorry about everything too. But instead, Doug told me that his wife, who had been a friend of Ted's late first wife, had dreamed that Evelyn in Heaven was laughing at my predicament. I was stunned. Doug's voice was icy. I felt sick. And I knew no one else who could possibly intercede to help me.

I prayed that Ted would have cooled off and wouldn't want to lose me. I thought that because of our issues with the boys, we were just going through a rough patch, and that we still truly loved each other. I called but he wouldn't pick up at home or take my calls at his office.

Reluctantly, I hired the attorney Carol recommended. I told him I just wanted marriage counseling, but when he contacted him, Ted said he didn't want counseling, he wanted a divorce. I was devastated that I had created this catastrophe. I thought it was all my fault. One of the only times in my life I had expressed my anger and look what it brought. But it was all a set-up.

In my rush to leave the house that night, when I told Jenny to pack up her schoolbooks, she rebelled.

"No! I want to stay with Daddy!" she cried.

And of course, I told her no, that she was coming with me. Thank God I insisted so she could blame it on me. If I had said "Fine! Stay here, I'm leaving!" she might have had to hear Ted saying "No, you're not staying here! Go with your mother." And that would have been two Daddies abandoning her, this one to her face.

I saw what an enormous mistake my ultimatum at the restaurant had been. Somehow, I had thought I was standing in my power when I said it. And I thought that his agreement to marry me, rather than lose me, meant he would not begin dating other women. I had no idea that he had at least one other woman already. What he had done was so unlike the person I thought he was. I could never imagine myself betraying him, or anyone.

When we were first married, I gave my car to the boys. And Ted, who had the 14 vintage sports cars, always drove the *Cutlass* to work. (Remember?) That left the gorgeous red Corvette convertible to me, which is what I had been driving to the grocery store and to my painting classes. So of course, that's what I drove when I stormed out of the house, crying, with Jenny in tow and a hastily packed suitcase, to rush across the street to my friend Carol.

The next day I drove the Corvette downtown when I went to ask for Doug's help. However, the following morning, when I went out to get in the car, it wouldn't start. It was the one and only time I was able to reach Ted, who said he would have it hauled away, and rent a car for me.

That afternoon an ugly little green Pinto (*extinct now, but you can Google it*) was brought to replace it. It could not have been further toward the opposite end of the vehicle spectrum. A slap in the face, back at me. Of course, I had no doubt that Ted had just disengaged the starter in the dark of night so he could reclaim his fabulous red Corvette.

I was heartsick and scared. I had lost everything: my dreams, my joy, my marriage, and I'd given up my job. By now I had been a fashion illustrator in the advertising department at every department store in town. Where could I go now? I had to create a new home for Jenny and me. And once again, I had taken her away from a Daddy. She never talked about him, or about what was happening to our lives. Maybe my own feelings were bleeding all over her. She didn't say, so I didn't know. Once again, I was incredibly sorry. And determined to build a new and happier life for us. However, as always, I had no money. Not a cent.

I needed a job, and I also desperately needed answers. Carol told me about a course called Silva Mind Control (now called The Silva Method) about how to develop your intuition, your psychic awareness. We both signed up and I quickly found I was very good at this. Another woman taking the class, Dr. Jackie Suggs, was a numerologist and had studied with John Macri, the man who had given me a quick reading of my chart at the Halloween party the year before.

Jackie gave me a much longer reading than he had. What I saw in my chart was such an affirmation of who I hoped I was, who I secretly thought I was, and who I prayed to become.

There was my creativity, my eagerness for adventure, even my longing to discover deeper spiritual connection! I was so astonished at the insight Numerology could reveal that I had to learn how to do this myself. At last, I was accessing some of the Mysteries I sensed were out there to be discovered. I begged Jackie to teach me.

From the day I began studying with her, I started to read for my friends too. Even as I continued with my art career, my work as a numerologist became even more important to me, helping other people connect to the power of their own soul's blueprint.

Seeing and understanding my chart was like walking through a door that had swung open to show me the path to my life's purpose and fulfillment. I saw that I inherently already held the qualities, the strengths, and gifts that I had always most wanted to have and to develop. There was my soul that longs to create and entertain, my ability to study and to teach what I love to learn, my gift of bringing in a Vision. There was also a Karmic Lesson, or Focus. My karma is with marriage and family. Of course! That is totally everything my life has been about from the beginning. It's taken years of living through life's lessons, with its successes and failures, and one especially extraordinary journey, to begin to truly understand and then step into the strength and the power of my chart.

I could hardly wait to see what Jenny's chart would hold. What gifts she has! What opportunities await! I was thrilled for her. It holds much more potential power than my own. And there was so much within it that echoed mine, especially in a focus on her creative gifts. Her karma is around work; hopefully that will be less painful than my own, dealing with marriage and family. It was fascinating to see that she was born with an

Expression number that matches my Life Path number, so she is a teacher to me. And that has certainly become a profound truth.

In the meantime, the only thing I could do, once more, was to ask for my old job back, now at a different store than the one where my darling Gilbert had worked, for by this time he had moved to Houston. I had another dear boss who kindly brought me back on board. But there was a hitch. Though I would earn my old salary, I had to share the responsibilities with the man he had hired to replace me when I left.

That sounded agreeable. Then I learned that my new advertising co-director was the man who had introduced my soon-to-be-ex-husband to the woman he moved into our house with her baby *(and his?)* just three weeks after I left. Ted married her six months later, the day after our divorce was final. Only later did I realize she was also the artist who had replaced me when I left the store to marry the man who would, so soon, become her husband too. The only piece of this sordid story that soothed me was that I was, by far, the better artist. Small comfort.

And that was about all I got when the divorce was final. During our marriage, Ted had begun proceedings to adopt Jenny, so it was determined that he would pay $375 @ month in child support. I received nothing beyond a few thousand dollars to replace the car I brought into the marriage and had given to Terry and Tim.

So, my husband married two brides in 16 months. The worst part? I still thought I loved him and ached with missing those first six years with him for a long, long time. Eventually, thankfully, I realized it wasn't really Ted that I missed; after all, he'd been an unfaithful snake to me, just as he'd been to Evelyn *with* me. She probably *was* happy to see me get my comeuppance. No, what I really missed was the sexually fulfilled me, and the me that believed we were both in love. Realizing this finally helped me heal this heartbreak. But still, it took years.

Of course, my new "colleague" was unbearable. I had met him and his wife once before with Ted, when we had all gone to dinner together. I didn't like him then, and I couldn't stand him now. The feeling was obviously mutual because he made no effort to be cordial. To add to my discomfort, my wonderful boss left to take a job in another city, and his replacement was a younger man who was not a fan of women in business. Still, I had to tough it out. I needed the money.

Then, a ray of light: I began to get a few portrait commissions on the side. Buoyed with confidence from the flattering attention I received, I decided to leave this job where I was always defending myself against these ill-tempered men, to become a self-employed portrait artist. That seemed plausible for several months, just long enough to paint three commissions, until I had to admit to myself that I had no idea how to get more. I was forced to look at what must have been obvious to all who knew me, I couldn't depend on this to support us. This seems to have been my most ill-thought-out plan ever. But wait, there's more! Another one is coming up later in another town and it will cost me much more.

I'm astounded now to relive these follies of mine and realize how foolish they were, even though they all seemed to me to be great ideas at the time. And I don't remember any friends suggesting otherwise. (Like, "Are you NUTS?") I know I wasn't, but I was incredibly foolhardy.

Years later a friend kindly made it clear to me that it was "magical thinking". For a long time, I guess I thought that my energy, my talent, my optimism, and my adventurous spirit would always see me through to find yet another job.

This time I quickly had to find one, but by now I had worked everywhere in this city. I had to cast a wider net. I was also eager to leave town for another reason. I didn't want to run into Ted and his new wife and baby anywhere. Especially the baby; that would be unbearable.

I began sending inquiries to department stores and ad agencies in various cities. Not pining for New York any longer, just for any place that would take me. Of course, this was long before the internet, so I had only the slow process of using the U.S. Mail. It was especially unfortunate timing as there was a recession affecting most of the country, and jobs were scarce.

But finally, a miracle! I was invited to come to Salt Lake

City for an interview to become the Art Director in the advertising department at the most prestigious store in town, the one that had been founded by Brigham Young shortly after he founded Salt Lake City itself in 1868. And if they gave me the job, they would pay for my furniture to be moved!

Hallelujah! Salvation might be at hand!

Nineteen
Searching Out: Salt Lake City, Las Vegas 1975 - 77

They gave me a good offer and I jumped at it! What an adventure it was for Jenny and me, leaving the flatlands of the Midwest as we made the drive out there. I began to feel hope that we could leave the past behind and start over, creating new lives for ourselves that would be better than ever.

I had never been west of the Mississippi, except to fly over it on the way to California. Once we got past Kansas, what a changing landscape with mountains in all directions, off in the distance. Everywhere were views I'd only seen in travel magazines.

As soon as we left the city limits of Cheyenne, Wyoming, we found we were perched atop an enormous mountain. I hadn't even realized we had been steadily climbing a little higher with each mile. Beginning the steep ride down took my breath away.

"Look!" Jenny pointed. "That sign says, 'RUNAWAY TRUCKS USE LEFT LANE'".

Holy Cow! Trucks can run AWAY? But I tried to stay calm so Jenny wouldn't be alarmed.

I kept my eyes darting back and forth from the road to my rear-view mirror, praying there weren't any trucks beginning to lose it. Then I saw that the left lane allowed them to ease off onto a soft grassy meridian that eventually leveled flat in a literal last-ditch effort to stop them.

What a jolt to see the price one had to pay for glorious scenery like this. I have no idea how long I held my breath. And that was just the first big mountain.

That winter in Utah, the snow brought unimaginable beauty. The streets must have been heated under the pavement, so they were dry and clear and the thick snow that was covering the lawns and the roofs of the houses made a scene like a Christmas card. After negotiating the icy slush in the streets in Indianapolis for so many years, this dry air was magic to me.

We settled in. Jenny began middle school, and I began my new job. The people in the advertising department were as friendly and welcoming as I have always found ad folks to be. I had an office of my own with a door, not just a cubicle.

One day I had a message from my nice new boss. *I've always been lucky that way, haven't I? And so thankful.* He called me into his office and closed the door.

Dick Peters was a staunch member of the Mormon church, and he reminded me that this store had been founded by Brigham Young, who had led the original Mormons to Utah and founded not only this store, but Salt Lake City itself. Friends of mine in Indianapolis had asked me if I was concerned about moving to live among the Mormons, which had sounded very critical to me, even though I didn't have any idea what they were hinting at. I knew nothing about their religion, but I didn't have any prejudices about any religion, so I was sure I would be fine.

However.

Mr. Peters told me something that he had omitted during my in-person interview, that the religion was quite conservative, and that they didn't tolerate alcohol, coffee, tea, or tobacco (or other drugs, of course, like cola soda pop).

Therefore:

I wasn't allowed to smoke in my office. Oh. *No.* I'd been smoking at least two packs of cigarettes a day for years. Back then, everyone I knew smoked and always in their offices. Especially everyone in advertising, with the stress of daily deadlines for the newspaper ads. It never entered my mind that no one else in this office was smoking. I never noticed.

I couldn't even imagine quitting smoking. How would I draw? How would I do anything? I also couldn't imagine leaving this job that was totally saving Jenny and me.

I had to think quickly.

"Mr. Peters. Dick. I was smoking when you interviewed me here in your office. If you'd told me then that I wouldn't be allowed to smoke, I wouldn't have been able to accept your wonderful offer. Could we find a compromise? What if I keep my door closed? Would that work?"

Thankfully he must not have wanted to lose me.

"Yes, I think we can make that work", he said.

Whew.

Now I had plenty of visitors in my office all day long, making me wonder how I ever got my work done. I imagine that some of the staff who didn't smoke and probably hated the smell of it, must have thought it served me right when I nearly died from viral pneumonia later that year.

I had fallen ill shortly after arriving at the office that morning. I hadn't even gotten to my desk, but was standing in an open area, chatting with others, and feeling perfectly normal, when it came on so suddenly, it was as if someone had kicked me in the back of my knees. They began to buckle.

I knew I needed to turn around and drive back home while I was still able. Thinking I had the flu or a terrible cold, I called a doctor for some prescription cough medicine, which a pharmacy delivered. When Jenny got off the school bus that afternoon, I told her not to come near me, as I was probably contagious. I lay in bed in my room, too miserable to even entertain myself with a book. (*Reminding you again, this was lightyears before mobile phones or I'm sure I would have been checking my messages.*)

All of a sudden, I could not take my next breath. I ran to Jenny's room next to mine and managed to gasp "Call an ambulance." I don't even remember the paramedics coming or the ride to the hospital. It was the fourth time Jenny saved my life.

She was 12 years old and in the 7th grade now. For the first time ever, she flew alone to visit her father. She had only met him once before when she was five years old, when we traveled to St. Louis to visit Jack, who was in town from California visiting his mother, Helen.

Jenny was gone for a week, and I barely slept the entire time. I was afraid she would be so charmed by his stories that she would come home, hating me for having deprived her of a fabulous, fascinating father. But when I went to pick her up at the airport, I began to relax a little.

"It's a good thing you left him when you did," she said. "He's not very nice to women."

What a mixture of emotions this brought me. I felt relieved that she wasn't angry with me, but sad for her that Jack hadn't seemed like the loving father I'd prayed for, after losing the father I'd once hoped Ted would become.

I found wonderful people to enjoy in Salt Lake, both as colleagues and friends, but I didn't meet any men who attracted me. For once, I wasn't in love with a man, but I began falling in love with my new life. I focused on enjoying my time with Jenny, my creative work, and my friends. I even began taking piano lessons for the first time in my life. How I loved the spectacular beauty of the mountains. I had never seen a landscape so majestic.

Snowbird was the closest ski area to Salt Lake City and is incredibly beautiful. Unfortunately, I didn't realize until years after I'd moved away, that there was a ski school and that you could begin on bunny slopes. I knew a lot of people here who skied, and I just assumed that they were taught by their parents as children, when they were short and closer to the ground. Then I met another woman who'd moved here from the Midwest. After getting her properly outfitted, strapping on her skis and handing her the poles, her brother put her on a ski lift to the top of Snowbird. When they arrived, he gave her a little shove, then raced on passed her, saying he'd see her at the bottom, leaving her to figure it out for herself. She finally made it all the way down in profound terror, and never went back. I thought, *If that's how it's done, I don't have the guts.* I content myself with watching the Olympics when they follow a skier on a long curving downhill run, and just imagine what it must feel like.

Driving up to Snowbird with Jenny on Sunday afternoons, meeting with friends for brunch, it was fun watching other people ski through the enormous windows that look out onto the slopes.

But driving alone down the mountain one Sunday when Jenny had gone to a friend's house for the afternoon, I slid into the parking lot of a drugstore at the base of the mountain and found I had burned out my brakes, riding them the whole way down the steep descent. Happily, though, I had made it all the way into the parking lot without running into another car ahead of me and sending both of us flying off the mountain. Divine intervention? It felt like it.

After the first year at Brigham Young's store ZCMI, I was hired away, still in Salt Lake City, by a wealthy entrepreneur who had built a new boutique fashion store. I created some of the best fashion advertising of my entire career there, directing fabulous photo shoots with a terrific photographer, stunning-looking local models, and witty copy created by a wonderful copywriter who had left ZCMI with me. It was great fun until seven months later when I was fired the day after Christmas, discovering only later that my boss had been sleeping with my secretary and he wanted her to be the Advertising Director. Now *I* was screwed. Not even a severance package. The only truly awful boss I ever had.

Living on unemployment, I felt such a failure at 36. There were long months of having to figure out what I could buy at the grocery store that would feed the two of us for a week. Unemployment checks forced me into the tightest budget I had ever had.

Now I was desperate to get out of Salt Lake City, which in those days, felt like the country's smallest advertising market. There were no other fashion advertising jobs for me here. And for a while, no one would even respond to my inquiries, sent once again, in the US Mail.

Occasionally I picked up a few small freelance jobs, but they were far between. While I waited for the mail to bring me news of possible job offers, fingers crossed, I read a fascinating book about reincarnation by Dick Sutphen, *You Were Born Again To Be Together*. Somehow, I learned that he was going to be giving a lecture in Las Vegas, and I wanted to go. A little extra freelance money made it possible.

The Mysteries! For so long I had been looking for this kind of esoteric information, without really knowing what it meant, where it could lead, or what I could learn that would somehow help me. The idea of reincarnation had been calling to me ever since Jenny had first told me that she remembered being born. Then again, with greater urgency, when she said she'd known me when we were friends as little girls in this lifetime, and that she had later died. That memory had surfaced for her when she saw a particular photo of me at age seven in my mother's photo album.

But the story that I felt was the most important for me to understand, was when she told me how much better she liked it when *she* was the Mother and *I* was the Little Girl. From the moment she told me about that lifetime, it seemed to have brought forth an anger that never left her.

I called a woman who had recently given me my first astrology reading. She was game to come with me to Las Vegas for the weekend to check this fellow out. And Jenny got to spend the weekend with her best friend.

During the six-hour Greyhound bus ride we weren't allowed to smoke on board until we crossed the state line into Nevada. No smoking on busses in Utah. Same bus, same people, okay in Nevada. We arrived at a Hotel/Casino and checked into our rooms, then found the lecture located in a ballroom already filling with people. After talking awhile to explain the agenda, Mr. Sutphen released us for dinner, encouraging us to return with a pillow to prepare for a long evening where he would be regressing all of us in the entire ballroom into some of our past lives.

Returning there later, I was in awe of what we might be about to experience. First, he hypnotized everyone in the room for several minutes. When he woke us, he said that his assistants had been walking through the crowd looking for people who were obviously in a deeper trance than others. It felt fascinating to be that relaxed and I *had* seen glimpses of places and people he had guided us to find while we were "under," but I didn't feel I'd gone as deep as I imagined a trance might be.

He selected six people to join him on stage, seating them several feet apart from each other and one by one he instantly hypnotized each. When they were all under, he would tap someone's forehead and ask them questions about a past life; specifically guiding them toward the end of it. Goosebumps! Their voices changed. Some spoke with accents, or simply in a lower register. The stories they told were hair-raising. And he was just getting started!

Next, he chose one of the women and hypnotized her for two and half hours. As she spoke, a gripping story began to unravel of a lifetime when she was a young Jewish woman during the Second World War in Germany. She said that to save her life and the lives of her parents, she became the mistress of a German soldier. It was a harrowing tale, too sad to retell here, and ended in her death at the hands of the soldier she'd finally betrayed. When Sutphen woke her up, she recalled the entire session and said she was so thankful, that it had explained so much about her current life.

On the bus trip back to Salt Lake City, I thought deeply about reincarnation and was determined to find even more information. What did reincarnation have to do with this life? I hadn't yet learned enough about karma. I had been doing numerology readings for two years and there were so many more *Mysteries*

that I was longing to uncover. I wanted so much to understand what was happening with Jenny, and why the tone of our life together was changing from the loving connection that we had before. Her angry attitude toward me was only intensifying.

When I got home, I opened the front door and picked up the mail from the floor. There was a letter from a major department store in Dallas inviting me for an interview as the possible new Advertising Creative Director.

I flew there the following week, and they hired me that day. How thrilling to be moving to a much bigger city with a large advertising market. I knew I would have so many more opportunities available if I needed them beyond this one.

They paid for our move, even having my car hauled in the moving van, so that we could fly to Dallas. They also paid for the flight, and thankfully, they paid for our hotel room for a few days until the moving van arrived.

How fabulous. A new life. I would have an income again. I was deeply grateful.

Twenty
SPINNING OUT: Of control, Jenny in Dallas 1977-1996

Dallas!! In the beginning it looked a lot like the nighttime TV soap opera of the same name. There really were men everywhere wearing cowboy hats and cowboy boots, even with their business suits. The women then had big hair too, just as they did in the show.

Texas has been the friendliest place I've ever lived. When I began my wonderful new job as the creative director, I met Barbara, one of the art directors on my staff in the advertising department, and a real Texan. She quickly became my first friend, showing me around town. To start off, she introduced me to Tex-Mex food (the best!), taking me for lunch at Tolbert's Chili Parlor which had sawdust on the floor. It was right downtown only a few blocks from our store.

There was such a feeling of wide-open spaces (the sky really is bigger here) with more room to stretch and grow professionally and personally and with less social judgment than I'd known in Utah or growing up in the Midwest. From the beginning I've felt that anyone could become anything here, live any way one wanted to, be ambitious or laid back, because it seemed that Texans were so tolerant of other people's choices. This was such a breath of fresh hope, and it was helping me heal some of the pain I still carried from losing Ted.

My new job was a step up from my art direction and fashion illustration assignments and involved continual fashion photography shoots, which I loved directing. Life was on the upswing. In that moment, I couldn't imagine that a darker time was coming.

This was the year Jenny began high school. I was at a fashion photo shoot working with photographers I'd just met that day, when my office called to tell me that Jenny had been arrested and taken downtown to the police station. She was busted at 10 a.m., along with her teacher, for smoking pot in the school yard during recess. And this was only the first week of school.

I was shocked, scared, and angry. I had no idea how to handle this. One of the photographers who was framing a shot, heard me talking and took a break to give me the name of an attorney. He said I would need one and I phoned the number right away. Immediately all the memories of anguish I had gone through over Ted's refusal to deal with Tim's drug habit washed over me. I told the attorney that I didn't want Jenny to be released immediately. I certainly didn't want her to spend the night there, but I did want her to sit downtown all day, until 5 o'clock. I thought that jail would be a sobering experience. Wishful thinking, I know, but I hoped that she would be frightened enough not to smoke pot again.

You're probably already howling with laughter. But this was 1977. Marijuana was highly illegal, and I was frightened for her. I had seen how strung-out and withdrawn Tim had been. And Jenny seemed to be moving further away from me all the time. I couldn't bear for her to disappear down a rabbit hole with drugs.

From then on, even though I never saw it, smelled it, or knew how she got it – I felt sure her pot use continued. Maybe there were other drugs; who knows? I could glean nothing from her. I only knew that her increasing anger and sullen behavior, and my frustration over not knowing how to help her, meant ongoing pain for both of us.

We plodded on through her high school years. Anger begets anger. We railed at each other. In tears, unable to understand what was tearing us apart, I yelled at her.

"I feel like you've killed my innocent child, the little girl I loved so much! Why??"

"I can read you like a book, but you'll never know me!" Jenny spit back.

I suppose I was an open book because I had nothing to hide. And she must have had plenty to keep from me. As she promised, I'd never know.

I couldn't imagine why she acted like this. And then I realized that was the problem. I couldn't *imagine*. I couldn't see life through her eyes. I could not picture or understand why she was like she was. Why was she so angry, so uncommunicative?

The sullenness had been building during her years in middle school, but now her anger was taking her somewhere beyond me. I was helpless to reach her.

Jenny seemed to have no need for me, and no interest in anything; no ambition, no dreams for herself, that she shared with me, anyway. She appeared to have few friends, virtually no social life that I knew about. It was breaking my heart to see the light leave her eyes, her laughter gone. How was it possible to just watch her retreat and be unable to pull her back?

I was frightened for her, I was angry with her, I tried to reason with her. I told her that smoking pot, or whatever she was doing, was changing the way she was being in the world. When I had argued with Ted about Tim's drug habit, I knew I could never bear to see this happen to Jenny.

And now it was.

Desperate now, I called Ted, hoping he could give me some advice to help her. Hoping that by now he had finally faced Tim's addiction and had found a way to help him stop. I prayed that he would talk to her, and that she would listen. But even though he had begun the adoption process for Jenny during our brief marriage, he had the adoption rescinded later and the child support ended. She wasn't his daughter, so Ted had no interest in helping either of us.

I learned that one of Jenny's friends was on drugs, and after she had slit her wrists, her parents had sent her to a place for rehabilitation. They said it was a lock-down, and I just couldn't imagine sending Jenny there. These days, there are rehabs everywhere, and the internet has all kinds of information for parents who want to help their children. But back then, we were living in a different time, and I was at a loss.

I began dragging us through a series of individual sessions with various therapists, searching for answers and a way to heal this terrible energy that was eroding the love between us. This seemed so much worse than ordinary teenage rebellion. It felt like a darkness was closing in.

I searched for self-help books. I first discovered them when I was in high school in the 1950's and my parents were reading them. My mother was absorbed in *The Power of Positive Thinking* by Norman Vincent Peale. And my father was reading Dale Carnegie's *How to Win Friends & Influence People*. He frequently read Mary Baker Eddy's book on Christian Science, and he joined the Masons, and spent evenings reading their books. Looking for help this way felt natural to me.

I began studying with various spiritual teachers and took a course in astrology trying to understand what insight the skies could offer. I went to Native American sweat lodges and participated in ceremonies. I joined women's spiritual study groups. I found the Eastern Indian guru Amma, known everywhere as the hugging saint, who traveled the world and came to Dallas every Spring, each year holding me tenderly in her embrace, and bringing me comfort.

One of the early therapists I found told me that I had all the earmarks of an adult child of an alcoholic. She didn't enumerate what those earmarks were, and I was too startled to ask. I couldn't imagine that my father was an alcoholic, though he had a can of beer in his hand every evening after work. But he wasn't drunk. He always had a job. He was kind and he loved me. That was all I needed to know.

But when I began writing this book, I thought maybe I should look that up online. What were those earmarks, anyway?

Well, here they are - and she was right.

The Earmarks of An Adult Child of an Alcoholic:

- Difficulty standing up for yourself: *Yes, I felt guilty being here.*
- Problems with relationships: *Yes, as my story will continue to reveal.*
- Inability to have fun: *Yes, I feel guilty relaxing or playing games, even reading, unless it's 'research.'*
- Isolation: *Yes, I love seeing my friends, but I need a lot of time to myself.*
- Extreme Self-Criticism: *I'm better now. No, I'm not.*
- Feelings of depression & anxiety: *Some anxiety, even fear, no more depression.*
- Fear of abandonment: *No, because I leave first.*

- Avoidance of conflict: *Always, unless I'm ready to walk out.*
- Becoming an approval seeker: *Sadly, yes.*
- Frightened of angry people: *Yes, this too.*
- Terrified of personal criticism: *Yes, it feels like welts on my back, just like the welts on my legs from my mother's switchings.*
- Constantly aim for approval: *Yes, if I do well, I get to stay another day; my ticket to ride.*
- Problems with project completion: *Yes, so why did I choose a career with deadlines?*
- Rescuer: *Only briefly, now.*
- Very loyal: *Yes, up to a point.*
- Frightened of authority figures: *Yes, always.*
- Addicted to excitement: *Yes – Travel! Movies! Sugar!*
- Live as a victim: *No - not anymore.*

Pity that I never went back to that therapist, thinking she was way off base, and didn't get me. I might have found some real insight for myself, and for Jenny, if I had.

I spoke to friends. They didn't have children who were angry like my daughter. They didn't know what to say. I still couldn't get through to Jenny and therapy didn't seem to be bringing her any relief either. Nothing changed. Nothing shifted. So nothing healed.

When she wasn't attacking me, Jenny was guarded. She still wouldn't engage in conversation to tell me why she was so angry with me. Was it because I had taken her away from two fathers? I never knew. Neither of us seemed capable of finding any joy in our life together. She was resentful, anxious, and manipulative. I was suspicious, anxious, and defensive. I felt drained, hated, and overwhelmed. Unable to make a difference, I walked on eggshells.

All the good times we'd shared long ago had vanished. I felt there was nothing I could do to reach her. And I missed her terribly, the child I'd so longed for and deeply loved.

Hoping a change of scene could shake us out of this mutual anguish and remembering the fabulous surprise trip to New York my parents had given me before my last year of high school, I thought I would create the same experience for Jenny. And like my parents had, I would tell her she could invite a friend to go with us. Sadly, she wasn't thrilled about this gift, not even mildly excited, but grudgingly said she would go, as if she were doing me a favor, and invited Beth, a nice girl I hadn't met before.

We flew to New York over Spring Break in her senior year. I made plans for us to go places I thought the girls would enjoy: a Broadway show, a visit to the United Nations and the Museum of Modern Art, shopping in the stores, restaurants with different foods, and lots of time to spend just walking around the city, marveling at it all. Of course, on the first night we'd go to Times Square, which I thought would be especially awesome to them, just as my first sight of it had been.

Despite all the opportunities to have fun and enjoy our trip, Jenny was just as gloomy and cross as she always was at home. I could see how uncomfortable and confused Beth was feeling with Jenny's rude behavior, but as usual, there was nothing I could say or do that would alter it. I was so disappointed that even having a friend along couldn't change her dark mood.

Finally, on the morning we were getting ready to go the United Nations, Jenny angrily refused to get out of bed. So, I said to Beth, "Let's just go on by ourselves! I think you'll be amazed by the U.N.!"

What a good time we had. What a lovely girl. What a blessed change to spend the afternoon enjoying each other's company, discovering something interesting together. I never saw her again. I imagine she was no longer interested in remaining friendly with Jenny. It was obvious when we were in New York that she was stunned by Jenny's behavior and sad for me, watching the disappointment I couldn't hide.

During her high school years, I told Jenny she would have to get good grades in order to get a scholarship, because I didn't have the money to send her to college; I was spending everything on therapy for both of us. But though she didn't flunk out, she never seemed interested enough to get the kind of grades I knew she was capable of, that would have given her the chance for a scholarship. I knew she was very smart. She had tested four years above her grade level in elementary school in mathematics. A class I always hated, which made me believe she was truly a genius.

By the fall after her graduation from high school, we were both several months into deep inner work in our respective therapy groups. Jenny had decided to enroll at a local junior college, and I was delighted that she appeared interested in her classes. She was still angry with me, but at least she was enjoying something. I was hopeful that she was moving out of her darkness, and that our relationship would improve, and we could one day be close again.

Then one morning while she was in class, I had a call from Nancy, our therapist.

"I need you to come to my office at one this afternoon," she said.

When I arrived, she told me that Jenny had been trying to talk one of the other young women in her therapy group into committing suicide.

"I've already reserved a bed for her at Methodist Hospital in the psych ward. I would like you to phone her and tell her you're here, and that we need to see her now. When I confront her with this, if she shows remorse, I believe that I can work with her. I will take her home with me for two weeks. If she doesn't show any emotion, I recommend that you have her committed for psychiatric evaluation."

I doubled over. What a horrendous accusation! What if it's true? I began howling, making terrible sounds, I'm sure, but I didn't care, and I couldn't have stopped myself if I had. It was like when I was in labor and couldn't even hear myself scream. My heart was shattering. Finally, when there was nothing left of me, and I was numb, I phoned Jenny and told her to come to Nancy's office immediately.

When she arrived, I sat facing her so I could watch her expression. She cried. I felt immediately that she wasn't crying from remorse, but from the shock of being found out by someone who wasn't beaten down by her anger like I was. But it was all Nancy needed. She told Jenny she was coming home with her. With great relief, I watched them leave together. It was a radical plan, but I trusted Nancy, and it felt preferable to sending her to a psych ward or to a lockdown rehab facility for troubled teens or drug addicts.

In my own session at the end of Jenny's first week in her home, Nancy talked frankly with me. "I strongly recommend that you find a place for her to live on her own that you can pay for, for six months, and tell her that during that time she will need to find a job to support herself."

I knew she was right. Something had to be done. This seemed monstrous, but for years I had found no way of reaching Jenny myself. Sick at the thought, but finally, without any other solution, I found a small studio apartment for her, about a ten-minute drive away. I had already given her my car instead of trading it in when I bought a new one. I moved all her possessions: her bedroom furniture, clothes, records, books.

I bought dishes and cups and glasses, pots and pans, and flatware. I signed a lease, paid the deposit and the first month's rent.

When Nancy said she was ready a week later, I took Jenny to her new apartment, and told her she would have to find a job to pay for it going forward, after the first six months. As expected, she was shocked and angrier than ever, but her choices had been removed. She found a job. I continued to pay for her therapy and mine.

Two or three years went by, Jenny had a succession of menial jobs, and then she moved in with a man she'd been seeing. The few times I saw them, they were high. She quit her job to make more money cleaning houses, which I was told is a typical gig for drug addicts. We seldom spoke. When I finally visited their apartment, it was filthy. When she told me she was pregnant and asked me for money for an abortion, I gave it to her. They were in no shape to have a child, who would surely have been born addicted, or worse.

A few months later, she called to tell me that he'd hit her, and she'd called the police. I drove to their apartment and found her sitting outside on a picnic table. He hung back away from us.

"Why is he still here?" I asked.

"Because I decided not to press charges," Jenny said.

I begged her to leave him and by the end of the week she did. She came to live again with me.

Soon after moving in, Jenny joined Narcotics Anonymous and got clean. One of the most important recommendations of the 12 Step programs is to not get into a new romantic relationship until you've had a year clean. But she quickly fell in love with another recovering addict who had also not yet had a full clean year.

At first it was such a relief to see her happy and laughing, with the light in her eyes that had been missing for so many years. We were no longer arguing, but she was very demanding and manipulative. I was relieved and grateful that she was clean and not overtly angry, but her energy was slippery, and I could never seem to lose the queasy feeling I had that I was being had. Just like the time when, although I couldn't afford it, I found myself agreeing to pay for much of her expensive wedding she'd planned to this young man who lost his humble dishwashing job the day before the elegant event.

Writing this chapter, I was ready to describe Jenny's wedding reception when I realized I had no memory of it at all. None. I've never been to a wedding without a reception, yet I could recall absolutely nothing. I phoned Larry, my long-time dear friend who I felt certainly must have attended Jenny's wedding.

Before I could even ask him about it, he began to reminisce about what a wonderful reception it was. He told me how happy I'd seemed, like an Auntie Mame, dancing the night away, waving my arms in the air with delight. I was stunned. I'd never imagined myself as having any skill at covering my true feelings. And I always thought I'd recalled every important detail in my life. To find my mind totally blank on this, makes me understand now how traumatized I'd been by my concern for Jenny's future with this young man I'd barely had time to get to know.

I had hoped my generosity would prove my love to Jenny, and that she would appreciate and love me in return, and the dark times would be over.

But then I've been the last one to see that she always held the reins in our relationship. Eventually I would realize how I'd always given up my power to everyone, not just to the men I married. To anyone I hoped would love me. Especially my child.

For the duration of their three-year marriage, I imagine Jenny supported him. And when the marriage was over, so was her abstinence from drugs.

Twenty-One
Making Out/ Falling Out:
Freelance / Brad / Bankrupt 1982-85

I needed more money. Therapy is expensive. I was finding it harder and harder to concentrate on my work at the ad agency. I was so upset with the constant arguing with Jenny, that I'd developed panic attacks, with adrenalin running up and down my spine while I was driving to work. My heart racing, I felt as if I couldn't breathe. I had no idea what was happening to me.

It was just about then that a guy at the ad agency whom I barely knew saw some of my layout sketches and made an offhand remark that I'd make a fortune if I went freelance doing storyboards for tv commercials. He said the whole 60-second spots were told in a series of 4 x 6-inch colored-marker sketches. The account execs would show these to the client to get the budget approved before shooting the commercial on location.

They would often follow these storyboards to the letter, so they had to be very good.

He told me the reason they paid so well was that they had to be turned over so quickly, often overnight, from the time the creative staff told the artist what the story was, till the time of the presentation to the client. Wow, intense. Then he said "Well, the burnout is huge! You can probably only stand it for a year." I lasted sixteen.

I loved the freedom of working at home, but the pressure! The all-nighters. And I hated every minute of the work. No fashion here. Lots of product shots with detailed logos precisely drawn. Inhaling the benzine from the colored markers and cranking it out six times faster than I'd done when I was in my ad agency office, nearly killed me. I was smoking way too many packs of non-filter cigarettes, staying up all night most nights, then managing to hand the finished work to a messenger service at my front door in the early a.m.

After a few hours' sleep I'd have breakfast, then go to the movies in the middle of the day in the middle of the week. My favorite indulgence.

I certainly did make a great deal more money, and I spent it as fast I as I made it. It had never occurred to me that the well could run dry, or that I couldn't keep cranking this out as long as I wanted to. Besides going to the movies, I went to the airport and flew off for mini vacations whenever I'd gotten a particularly large check.

The pressure was intense. Once while I was in the hospital for a week with a fractured pelvis from a car accident, I finished a big job sitting there surrounded with all my art supplies and a makeshift drawing board in my hospital bed.

I finally admitted that it was beginning to exhaust me. And one day I had an idea that I thought could change my trajectory.

At first it all seemed very possible when I thought of contacting an old friend who was doing well in, you guessed it, New York; that place that kept taking up so much space in my dreams for myself.

Brad was a younger friend who had been a college intern gofer several years earlier in the advertising department at one of the stores in Indianapolis where I was an illustrator. Not much later, he left for New York, and in a miraculously short time, it seemed to me, he was beginning to make a name for himself as a fashion designer, specializing in loungewear. Diana Ross and the Supremes had discovered him, and I'd seen a photo of them wearing his slinky jersey copper-colored gowns with beautiful matching ostrich feather jackets. His work was simple, dramatic and elegant. At this point, he didn't yet have his own company, but he did have his name on the label.

We had always loosely stayed in touch, and of course I was following the ad campaign for his designs in the fashion press, full page ads with full color photographs in "W" for each design. I just knew I could create even more beautiful ads for him with even more exciting photography, so I contacted him and told him my great idea: I'd come to New York to pitch his account.

Brad said he wasn't happy with his campaigns, but he had no clout within the company to make those decisions. He encouraged me to come but told me he couldn't even sit in on the presentation because the owners, two old and very conservative, very straight men resented having to work with him, since he was a very out and effeminate gay man. He said that if he recommended me, it would be an immediate turnoff for them. They needed him, but they didn't like him, he said. I would do much better on my own.

In addition to my fashion illustration, I had also been art directing fashion photography for quite a while by then and had recently been working with a photographer who had developed an edgy technique, very slightly moving the camera while he grabbed a shot. At the time, it was unique and added a sensual urgency to the photos. Today it would be so easy to create that electronically, and an endless series of other effects, but back then it looked so avant-garde!

Brad gave me the contact information and right away I was able to get an appointment to pitch my presentation to these men. I was so excited to know that I could put together a fabulous collection of ads using this gorgeous technique, and I was sure I had a very real chance to land their account.

I had all the confidence in the world in my concept, my taste, and my design ability, and I loved art directing fashion photography. I had so many wonderful friends in the business; the photographer offered his services gratis, the models and makeup artists did too. Everyone was behind me in putting this together.

Of course, while they offered to work with me on this project for free, I had to work around everyone's else's shooting schedules, they couldn't drop paying work for me. So, I had to be ready at a moment's notice, therefore unable to accept any of my own lucrative freelance work. My bills and my credit card balances soared, and my bank balance dwindled to dust.

But finally, after months of working around everyone else's availability, I had 5 beautiful ads that I thought would knock their socks off, even in New York!

Feeling it was the least he could do for me, I even enlisted Ted's help, telling him what I was trying to do, and asking him if he would produce large plastic-coated prints of the ads, mounted on foam-core for me to take to the presentation, and he agreed. I sent him the film and flew to Indianapolis to fetch the samples when they were ready. I had a lump in my throat, seeing him again after all these years. I knew it wouldn't be easy, but I needed his help to make this a truly professional presentation. And the ads were exquisite, making me feel sure I could pull this off, becoming an ad agency owner and bringing in a New York client.

I brought these fabulous mock-ups home and got my best clothes ready for the momentous trip to New York, where once again, I believed my dreams could come true. I thought that this time I had finally found the key that would do it.

And, betting on these yet-to-unfold good times coming, I had signed a lease on some very expensive office space so I could become a legit fashion ad agency, even planning on hiring some of my dearest friends to staff up. Here in Texas, leases are unbreakable. Unless, of course, you file bankruptcy.

The morning came to board the plane and I woke up feeling violently ill. I hadn't been nervous the night before, so I was certain that this wasn't simply fear– that I must have a bad virus. But I had to get to the airport. Everything was riding on this.

Thankfully the flight was smooth and before long I landed at LaGuardia in New Jersey and got a cab into the city. I checked into the hotel Brad recommended. And two hours later, still feeling weak in the knees, I went to the Garment Center address and made my presentation to two unsmiling men who seemed surprisingly unsophisticated.

They owned a company that for years had only made what used to be called housedresses or dusters, sort of shapeless flower-printed cotton numbers that zipped up the front. I would never have been caught dead in one. How they had the foresight to transition over to beautiful loungewear was beyond my imagining. Their manner was expressionless and flat, totally unwelcoming and seemingly uninterested. I was surprised they had even let me make the appointment.

But that all changed when they saw my work. I knew that

both the photography and the design of my ads were far more exciting than the ones they were running in the fashion press, even though they had been shooting them with a well-known photographer. Then these two men, looking at me with suspicion, asked: "How did you do that?" referring to the stunning effect of the photography. They didn't seem like they wanted to hire me, just to steal from me. So I didn't tell them how I did it. But I did invite them to come to my office in Dallas (the empty one I had just leased) since they were already planning to be there for the fashion market the following week. Surprisingly, they showed up.

They walked into the office building that was still under construction and then into my office which was ditto. What was I thinking to invite them here? I had nothing to show them beyond what I had brought to New York. No other campaigns, no other fashion clients, no employees. I wasn't even listed in the phone book as an ad agency.

The facade I had tried to pull off in New York, of being a savvy advertising maven, was gone. With their arrival, I was suddenly snapped out of the daydream I'd been in for months. Exposed. Mortified. I felt as revealed as I had been at age three when after falling off a swing and into a mud puddle in the park, my mother removed my sunsuit and rinsed it off in a water fountain, while I stood there naked.

The humiliation of feeling this ludicrous idea evaporate after all the time and money and effort I'd spent betting on my dream, was beyond describing. I remember nothing of our conversation. I'm sure it was mercifully short.

As I combed through files of old correspondence to write this chapter, I came across a lovely card that enclosed a riveting multi-page eulogy for my designer friend, who died much too young; a mere 10 years after my aborted presentation. I was shocked to read of his incredible successes. I saw that he had already achieved far more renown than I had been aware of back when he told me he didn't have the power to help me.

It turns out that Diana Ross and the Supremes weren't the only well-known women who loved his clothes. In addition to the honor of having Princess Grace wearing one of his creations when she hosted a royal tennis tournament in Monaco, it seems he was spending half the year in Hong Kong designing his collections when he was not at home in his Park Avenue apartment. There were details that he had found a following among First Ladies, Arabian princesses, wives of Washington powerbrokers, and movie and television stars. Some of the names dropped in this eight-page tribute: Pat Nixon, Nancy Reagan, the Maharani of Jaipur, on whose private train Brad had once traveled; Dina Merrill, Nancy Kissinger, Jaclyn Smith, Candice Bergen, and Britain's Princess Michael of Kent.

Oh, that stings. I am truly happy for him that he had such an illustrious career. I only wish he had been more direct and let me know that since he didn't want to put himself out to help me, that I didn't really have a chance. Maybe he did imply that, and I simply chose not to let it register.

When I finally faced that I had been living in LaLa-land all that time, I wondered how I could have been so naive, so unprofessional. Why hadn't I thought of asking myself some important questions, like, *"Should I build an agency first before I pitch a client?"* Now I began to understand the importance of what professional people call 'exercising due diligence' before taking risks. Surely, my friends and colleagues must have seen me racing at top speed toward a brick wall. But everyone I knew, even my therapist, was cheering me on.

Twenty-Two
Reaching Out: Travel Agent 1997

Here's another classic: "Well, back to the drawing board!" and that's exactly where I headed.

Calculating my overdue bills from those months of not doing the work that would have paid them, and deeply regretting having signed a lease I couldn't argue my way out of, I was quickly propelled into the nightmare of attorney's fees and bankruptcy. Because I was also behind with the IRS, I had to choose Chapter 13, paying it all off, instead of being able to walk away with a Chapter 7. This choked me with high payments for years.

But thankfully, it protected me from creditors while I was able to reclaim my clients and earn a living again. I was so thankful to be back on the drawing board that now even the benzene markers smelled sweet. I began painting portraits again, too, which was more creative for me personally and financially helped me immensely.

Even so, there was no longer enough money to be flying off anywhere after the big jobs were turned in. So of course, I came up with another Brilliant Idea. It occurred to me that I could take a short course at a travel agency and become a travel agent. Fabulous!

I reasoned that if I could convince groups of people to go on beautiful European jaunts, hosting them myself, it would cover my own expenses. It turned out that I was right: that's exactly how it works. I decided I would create a brochure on my new computer showing prospective clients all the places I would take them on a two- to three-week trip to Europe.

Since my freelance company was Lilypad Productions, I decided that my European trips would be handled by my Flying Frog Tours, jumping across the Pond.

My first thought was to make a pitch to art clubs, saying "Let's Go Paint In Italy"! To make it more specific I needed to create an itinerary, so I began asking for help from friends who were happy to offer ideas.

Dear Gilbert, my former art director and best boss ever, gave me the name of an Italian friend of his who was a chef: Francesco Lombardi in the town of Arezzo in Tuscany. He thought Francesco would be happy to give the group a cooking lesson. Brilliant! This was years before I began reading of others offering Italian cooking lessons to tourists. And because this was also a few years before the internet was popular, with people booking their own travel to Europe and beyond, travel agents were still helpful and often necessary.

I sent a letter to Mr. Lombardi at his home in Arezzo and he answered quickly that he was interested in the idea. I was on a roll. I told him I would be in Italy in July and would like to visit him to make further plans on my way to a workshop I would be taking in Umbria. He replied that he would be delighted to pick me up at the airport in Rome and drive me to Arezzo. Excellent! I felt I was already on my way to making this new dream a reality.

I chose a pastoral area near Florence where we could paint outdoors *en plein air* after visiting the famous museums in the city. Then I chose a winery in Tuscany that would give us a tour and a delicious lunch accompanied by different wines for each course. When I had all my ideas gathered, including a tour in Rome of St. Peter's Basilica and other ancient sites, I created an enticing two-week package, then added another optional week to continue north to Venice by train.

By now it was the middle of March, and I could hardly wait to show this to everyone. I planned to hand out the brochures describing all the details of my curated autumn journey, along with a presentation of photos of Italy that I had assembled in a portfolio of all the places I intended to take everyone. Off I went to the two local art clubs, full of excitement, certain that I would find enough people who would be eager to join me. I only needed twenty.

Why did I once again think that everything would go just as I imagine it? I could never seem to picture that it wouldn't. It was probably because of all the movies I loved, and their happy endings. I still hadn't got the hang of due diligence.

Well, it turned out that the artists who could afford to go were already booked to fly to Italy or Greece or France in September with nationally known painting instructors! I hadn't even thought of creating a *teaching* workshop. I was just assuming that since we all already knew how to paint, they would love my creative itinerary and be excited to pack up their paints and brushes and come along.

Based on my early confidence and enthusiasm, Frances, the woman who owned the travel agency, had already reserved a number of seats on the flight we planned to take. Now she told me that we had to have bookings guaranteed by a certain date or we wouldn't be able to go. We were going to have to advertise in the travel section of the Sunday newspaper, it was our only hope. We would just have to take whoever wanted to sign up with a deposit. So I let go of the idea of making time for painting; I had plenty of other wonderful plans for anyone we could get.

I was so grateful that Frances and her husband were planning to go with me, to show me the ropes of handling twenty people, getting them through customs and checking them into the hotels, counting noses to make sure they got on the appropriate buses at the correct times.

While the ad ran in the Sunday paper for the next few weeks, I was busy showing the brochure and the portfolio of photos to anyone who would stop to listen.

Book Three: Encore

Twenty-Three
Coming Out #2:
Falling For Grace -1997

One afternoon the studio phone rang, and the loveliest woman's voice asked, "Miss Stevens?"

I had never heard anyone address me with quite such gentleness and respect. This was definitely not a client, so what on earth could this woman be calling me about and why did she have this unusual sound to her voice? It gave me such pause that I will always remember that moment - where I was, and how I felt, hearing her say my name.

She told me her name was Grace and that she wanted to buy a painting of mine that was for sale at the restaurant where she had just been having lunch. I was thrilled: a freelance job I was counting on to cover the studio rent had just been cancelled earlier that day.

"How wonderful, thank you!" I said.

I was curious to hear which one she'd chosen, and I was

delighted when she told me. I remembered painting it and wondering who would select it.

Grace asked if I was available right then to receive her check. You bet! She arrived soon after and was just as gentle and kind as her voice. Of course, as she handed me the check, I handed her a brochure for my upcoming Italian adventure and began showing her the portfolio of enticing Italian photographs.

I offered her a seat on my studio's couch so she could easily look over the photos and read the details of the tour. She told me it sounded very interesting, and she thought the photos were inviting. She'd never been to Italy, only Greece, years before. She took the brochure with her, saying she'd like to come, and that she would bring me a deposit check the next day.

When she returned the following afternoon, we made plans to meet a week later when my show at the restaurant would end, and I would hand her the painting. On that day, as we ate lunch there, I told her how I had wondered who might buy that painting of a woman in the 1920's who was wearing a caftan and a cloche hat, whose eyes glanced down toward the bottom of the frame.

She told me that Grady, the owner of the Dream Cafe, had lost her order and she sat there for such a long time looking at the piece, just as the woman in the painting was looking down at her. Grace had recently bought a condo in the neighborhood so that she could stay the night in town when she worked late at her law office, and wouldn't have to drive back to her ranch, an hour away. Its walls were bare, and she thought the painting would be just what was needed. When Grady showed up at last with her food, apologizing for losing her order, she asked him if the painting was for sale. He told her yes, it was, adding "You'll like the artist, she's very different."

If this had taken place in these more recent days when we're all looking at our phones while we're waiting, I might never have sold this painting to Grace. She would have been checking her email. And this day that changed both our lives might never have happened.

While we were waiting for our lunch to arrive, I took out a piece of paper and a pen and asked her for her full name and birthdate. By this time, I'd been a numerologist and been teaching numerology for over 20 years. Not a day goes by without my doing a chart, whether it's for a client or someone I've read about or seen on television that I want to know more about. Of course, I always want to learn more about a person I like. And I already liked Grace very much.

First, she told me her name and as I wrote it out and decoded the numbers: *Shockabadeeda!* as my dear actress friend Elfriede would say. Grace's three most important name numbers matched my own! In all these years I had only seen that combination once, and it was a client's brother, a man I never met. A voice in my head *or my heart* said: "Pay attention. This woman is important in your life."

This must have been the first time I'd listened to what I now believe was either my guardian angel or one of my spirit guides. Whoever it was, they were finally getting my attention after all those years of my not noticing the red flags they were waving in the wind.

To add to that, our birthdays were only a week apart. Of course, reflecting her kind and gentle energy, Grace's Life Path was full of compassion and humanitarian presence. As an attorney specializing in eldercare, her work in the world exemplified everything I saw in her chart.

We became friends, going to lunches, movies, dinners. At the time, both of us were also seeing our own therapists to heal the wounds of our "inner child." We spoke the same language about what we were experiencing in our respective therapies.

I was beginning to have increasingly strong feelings for Grace. Finally, I admitted quietly to myself that I was falling in love with her. How could this be? I knew Grace was gay, but I wasn't. Still, it was true in my heart, I loved her. I was falling in love with her soul.

One evening after we had gone to a movie, I gave her a card I had found that said "My little girl loves your little girl" a play on the inner child idea, I thought, but also it spoke of love.

"Oh, how sweet," Grace said. *Oh no, she doesn't get it; that I really do love her. She just thinks it's a therapy term.*

I had always been accustomed to having men make the first move, after flirting with them and sending out signals to let them know how I felt, what I was thinking, and what I wanted them to do. Feeling love for a woman was different, and I tried to figure out how I needed to play it.

A few nights later, I saw I would just have to spell it out and tell her plainly how I felt. Grace told me then that she wouldn't have dared hope that I felt that way.

"My belief about straight women is that they might just be experimenting, and that for me to make a move, was a sure way to lose a good friend," she said. Once I made myself clear, she told me she already loved me too.

That night ended my confusion and began my fully expressed feelings with the most beautiful soul I have ever known. Just three months after we met, I gave up my apartment and moved in with Grace, to the condo where my painting was already installed.

By this time the Sunday newspaper ads in the travel section had brought in deposits from enough people to make our September trip to Italy a reality. We were excited to be planning it together and decided to take a class in conversational Italian that summer.

Before we met, I had already signed up for a singing workshop in Umbria. So barely a month after declaring our love for each other, I was off to the workshop for two weeks, carrying with me a stack of greeting cards from Grace to keep me company, and leaving a stack for her on the bedside table.

When I said goodbye to Grace, I flew from Dallas to New York on Continental Airlines, to change planes for Rome. I had very little time between flights, since the plane circled New York for nearly an hour before it landed. I had to run through the terminal to catch the Alitalia flight and I was certain that there was no way my luggage could have made it with me.

Very early the next morning when I arrived in Rome, Francesco Lombardi was there to meet me as promised. He had driven over two hours from his home in Arezzo. But I was nowhere to be seen. I was busy filling out forms to let the airline know my itinerary for the next week so that they could bring my missing bags to me when they would arrive in Rome, hopefully the next day.

Francesco was not in the best of moods when I finally emerged from Customs. Luckily, he had already sent me the name of the hotel where he would be taking me to spend the night. It was an ancient castle in Arezzo, so I had that address to give the airline. And amazingly one of my bags arrived there before I left the next day to catch the train for Perugia. I was happy to have my clothes and makeup and tooth-and hairbrushes. But where was my music? I had packed all of my song sheets in the other bag.

After getting me settled in at the Castello di Gargonza, Francesco took me to his home where he poured me a glass of wine and I watched as he created a sauce. It was simply a blend of olive oil, basil, garlic, onions, tomatoes, but they must have been freshly picked and the olives recently harvested. It was the most delicious sauce I have ever tasted. He tossed it around in a shallow pan over a fire, in that offhand manner chefs have of making it look easy.

When we sat down to dinner, several members of his family appeared, evidently curious to meet this Texas woman who wanted to bring people to Italy, an idea that was not so common then, 27 years ago. I had already sampled the fabulous dish I'd watched him prepare, and I could hardly wait to enjoy a big serving of it. When all ten of us were seated, and the wine was poured, an enormous bowl full of the sauce mixed with pasta was passed and after it had made the rounds, we all began eating. There was much laughter and such appreciation for the chef's cuisine.

I was asked if I would like some more. Of course I would, so a large serving bowl was passed to me. I put a lot more on my plate, it was so delicious. And then, just as I began stuffing more of it into my mouth, I looked up to see that everyone else had put their forks down, and all faces were turned toward me, watching me eat.

Horrors. What had I done? I had no idea that this incredible pasta dish might just be an appetizer! Growing up in the Midwest in the 1950s, everyone loved Italian food, but we thought it was so rich (and fattening) that we ate it only once a year, twice at most. And when we did, pasta was the main dish and the only other items on the table were bread and a green salad at the most wonderful Italian restaurant in town.

I couldn't imagine what would happen next. I wanted to finish eating this wonderful food, but I was embarrassed to continue while others just stared. I put my fork down. And then the fish course was served. Ooohs and ahhh all around. Minus mine. I can't even look at fish prepared to be eaten. Someone took away my lovely pasta. Oh no. And I couldn't possibly bring myself to try the fish. So now I just watched them eat, now with my fork down. I know they must have thought me a rube, a totally unsophisticated primitive from the wild West.

My impolite dining behavior may have contributed (along with his irritation at waiting so long for me to finish up at Customs in Rome) to Francesco's waning interest in creating a plan to teach cooking to my tour group. I was getting nervous that he wouldn't make a commitment, and now I had people coming in September who were expecting this! I returned to the Castello to spend the night, wondering how on earth I was going to make this promise of a cooking class work out. It was clear he could not be pinned down. I needed help.

The next morning, I caught the train to Perugia where the people who hosted the singing workshop met me with a van to transport me to their villa. The train ride was glorious. The hair-raising van ride up to their villa at the top of a steep mountain was frightening. But then - what a payoff! When we finally arrived, the most breathtaking view. I climbed out of the van and looked far out over the valleys and across to other high green mountains, dotted with more beautiful villas with horizon swimming pools and acres of lavender and roses. And there to greet me was my other bag with all my music in it, waiting for me in my room.

What a glorious setting! Locanda del Gallo near Gubbio, in Umbria. I'm telling you the name so you can find their website and see what a magnificent place this is. Heaven. I hope you will be able to visit there one day yourself.

Much of the fruits and vegetables they served, al fresco of course, in the beautiful summer weather, were grown on the property. The interiors were all created using Feng Shui, so the energy was beautifully balanced. The friendly and oh-so-talented teachers who assembled the workshop were from Israel, Germany, England, France, and the U.S. All were friends who had met years earlier at a theater workshop in Europe. They had created this event especially to gather together again every summer. It's called The Tuscany Project, and they're still holding it each year in this idyllic setting.

The hosts were Paola and Eric, who were charming and so helpful. I told Paola about my upcoming tour, and how I had promised to provide cooking lessons, which I now had no idea how I could pull off. She told me of her friend Donna, an American woman married to an Italian man, who could easily make it happen. While I was busy singing in class that afternoon, she phoned Donna who said she would be delighted to arrange it. What luck! I could hardly believe my good fortune; it felt like a miracle. I couldn't wait to tell Grace.

Twenty-Four
LEAPING OUT: Into Italy 1997

I became more than a singer here. For those two weeks, I became a performer. The teachers were total pros, inspiring, funny, and so supportive. The classes were exciting and boosted our confidence. The other 23 students had come from all over the world. They were delightful and so collaborative as we prepared to give a concert for the local village by the end of the two-week workshop.

On the weekend in between I took a train to Venice and checked into a cheap and tiny room that dear Gilbert had recommended. There was just enough space for a single bed and a wooden chair. But Gilbert assured me I wouldn't need anything more because I would be exploring Venice every waking moment. And he was right.

I spent divine hours on both evenings at the outdoor cafes with a glass of wine, listening to the music playing throughout the Piazza San Marco all evening long as the three orchestras took turns filling the air with romantic music.

On the long train ride back, I listened to a CD of Astor Piazzola's tangos playing in my ears continually, while gazing at the unending beauty of the Italian countryside.

By the close of those two glorious weeks, I was madly in love with Italy, reveling in this beautiful time-out-of-time experience with nothing to do beyond singing, enjoying these new friends, learning from these exciting and gifted teachers, eating delicious food and drinking in the beauty of the surroundings. I was already feeling impatient to return. I knew Grace would love it too and I couldn't wait to share it with her.

I had about two months to finalize plans before returning to Italy and Donna kept in touch with me, letting me know that she was on top of it.

Whatever would I have done without her? As it turned out, Donna did much more than I could have asked, creating an entire tour for us from our beginning in Rome to Florence and Tuscany. Grace and I returned in September with my travelers in tow, along with Frances, the travel agency owner and her husband. Each morning as we got on the tour bus, Donna handed each of us a copy of a terrific newsletter she'd whipped up on her computer the night before, explaining the day's itinerary, along with the history and current descriptions of the places we'd be seeing that day.

Of course it was magnificent, it was Italy! The scenery, the food, the history, the art and architecture, listening to the language; it was all a dream come true, beyond my imaginings when I'd first thought of it.

And the piece de resistance? Donna found Rory, a caterer who invited us into the kitchen at her own beautiful home on a lovely estate. She had us chopping vegetables, measuring ingredients, and learning how to cook in true Italian style every evening. For those four nights we made fresh pasta and the rest of the entire meal from scratch, before finally sitting down in the dining room along with her 94-year-old mother, to savor an incredible dinner at ten p.m.

Donna gave each of us a pretty full-length apron she'd had made by a woman in her village: 20 aprons, with our names stitched on in cursive. And Rory gave us each a plastic binder with printed recipes of everything we'd cooked each night.

I was so thankful to have Frances, my mentor, along on this adventure with her husband. They were enjoying it all too, while they showed me the ropes, guiding our people through customs, and making sure they were kept track of and kept safe as we traveled from one marvelous location to another.

When we got to Pompeii however, we had a problem. To tour the ancient city, we had to first climb over the awkward entrance, deeply rutted from ancient chariot wheels. One of the women in our group was in a wheelchair, traveling with her elderly husband. He was unable to lift her in the chair over the entrance and onto a flat street. Thankfully a strong young Italian man appeared from behind our group in line and was able to assist. But for him, we would have had to go somewhere else. We couldn't leave the couple behind while the rest of us spent the day in awe, climbing the rutted streets and examining the remaining houses and buildings in Pompeii.

By the time we had traveled a week, a few of those on the tour were getting a little irritated with a few of the others. Nerves were beginning to show; after all, some of these people had never been away from the United States. And I knew that sometimes people could become a little nervous and upset to be in a foreign land for the first time. I'd seen it before on other trips, but then I hadn't been the one to oversee anyone else's experience. Now I felt responsible for everyone's good time.

Some of the group had signed on for the optional week in Venice. Others would fly back to the States the following day. Our last excursion for the whole group was at the winery in Tuscany.

Here was the menu: Traditional Bruschetta, Pasta with Meat Sauce, Local Cheese, White Beans, and for dessert an Italian Fruit Pie "Crostata". Accompanying each course was a wine. First, it was Thesis, a white table wine. Next, Rosso di Montepulciano, a red wine. Then, Vino Nobile di Montepulciano, another red. Finished with Sangallo Vin Santo o Grappa.

The Grappa was 100 Proof. So, by the end of the meal, we were all laughing, crying, hugging one another, and vowing to stay in touch forever.

When we were in Rome at the beginning of our trip, Grace and I went shopping on the Via Condotti to buy wedding rings, even though at that time in the United States, we couldn't marry. That didn't matter to me; I was in love with her soul.

We arrived in Venice in the third and last week of our trip, and as soon as we found our little hotel and left our bags in our room, we walked to the enormous and ornate St. Mark's Basilica. The cathedral, whose multi-domed ceiling is lined in solid gold mosaics, was understandably filled with tourists.

There was no place we could see to stand off to ourselves, so there in the middle of all those people who were looking up at the ceiling and paying no attention to us, we gave each other our rings, both of us promising "I love you forever." We ducked back out into the immense beauty of the Piazza San Marco. It seemed the perfect ceremony, just the two of us, wedged into a magnificent setting with hundreds of other tourists. We followed it up with a frothy coffee and silky tiramisu at the elegant Caffe Florian, opened in 1720 and a favorite haunt of Casanova, Charles Dickens, and Ernest Hemingway over the years.

Later we joined the rest of the group that evening in the Piazza, enjoying our dinner al fresco while listening to those three orchestras as they each took their turns playing the romantic tunes that filled the enormous square.

Everything about that moment filled me all at once; the love I was feeling, the view of the people strolling by, the extraordinary architecture, the soft breezes of the autumn air, the marvelous food, and the beautiful music, soaring throughout the Piazza.

Everyone was thrilled with Venice, and even a week there wasn't enough. But finally, as all things must, it came to an end. This time, at last, my Big Idea was a grand success! And it paid for my trip, just as I'd prayed that it would.

Twenty-Five
Working It Out: Visiting Jenny
1999 –2015

Grace and I returned home to the details of our new life together. Meanwhile, Jenny. She liked Grace and seemed to be approving of our relationship. Finally, I was able to focus less on my daughter and more on my own life, my new happiness.

I experienced such validation with Grace. I fell against her shoulder, sitting on the couch one afternoon. Filled with relief, I let out a sob.

"I realize I've never had an advocate before," I said.

A few years after her divorce, Jenny moved to Colorado. She'd always been smart but had seemed unmotivated when she was younger. I was glad to hear that she was now taking college courses and getting increasingly better jobs. Her numerology chart indicated such powerful potential. I had great hope that she would be able to create a successful and happy life for herself. She got in on the early days of the tech industry and was a quick study.

But even though her life seemed to be improving, nothing changed in our relationship. She was still angry with me for reasons she would never share, hanging on to her now familiar hostility. I was still defensive and unable to find an easy conversation with her. I could only keep hoping that she would mellow with age and her increasing success.

Every few years, she would invite me for a visit. Of course, I always hoped she would be happy to see me. But the attacks and the anger continued. She was always on edge. Growing weary of her attitude, and never seeing any shift in sight, I would inevitably take my bag and leave her apartment building, going out to the street where I was glad to have a cellphone to call a taxi, once more off to the airport to catch a flight a day earlier than I'd planned.

Grace and I flew to Denver to visit Jenny for her birthday. I had created a photo album for her as a gift, enlarging many of my favorite snapshots of her over the years. As soon as she tore off the wrapping paper, opened the book and saw the photos, she threw it toward the floor, sailing it across the room, screaming that she hated her childhood.

"What has made you so hateful toward me all these years? Why won't you let me back in to your heart? Why do you keep punishing me? Is that why you invited us here, just to keep attacking me?"

That's what I wanted to scream back. Maybe I should have. Maybe the dam was ready to break, and I could have learned what the anger and resentment had been about all these years. But I say this with hindsight. When it happened, I was silent. I didn't want to make it any more unpleasant for Grace than it already was.

I could think of no way to respond to this outburst. It was another mind-fuck. As I had on every other visit, again I felt attacked, drained, unheard, disrespected, and overwhelmed by her rage. Each encounter broke my spirit further and made me feel even more hopeless that there could ever be a healing. In my lifetime I had never known anyone else who behaved like this, who would treat people this way.

Grace and I left the apartment; once again, I called a taxi and we left for the airport. On our way home I finally lost hope.

"Never again! I can't keep doing this, trying by myself to create the relationship I wish we had, to show her love when she's continually so angry with me. I can't find a way for us to be happy together, to just be *nice*. I can't fix what I don't even know is wrong."

I knew then that something had to change and realizing that therapy had done little to help me find answers, I began reading even more self-help books, which is how I found the spiritual teacher Debbie Ford. I picked up her first book *The Dark Side of The Light-Chasers*.

Reading it, I began to realize that because of my experiences with my intensely critical mother, especially her beating me for reasons I never understood, I was terrified of anger and desperate to please. I saw that because of that early imprint, my fear of judgment and criticism from anyone was monumental, especially any anger or criticism from Jenny.

I remembered how I had become frightened the minute I first saw the fuming, resentful expression on her face when she was five years old, telling me how much better she liked it when *she* was the Mother, and *I* was the Little Girl. The moment that awareness dawned on her, she seemed changed. The moment I felt her direct that energy to me, I gave her the power, and I gave up my own.

At last, I could see that this fear had never left me through all the therapies, seminars, courses, self-help books, workshops, and spiritual paths I had tried.

How I would love to be able to tell you that twenty years ago, after I learned all this, I took back my power, stopped taking a beating for things I hadn't done and began creating boundaries. But even though my awareness was evolving at the time, my ability to find the courage to change my own behavior was not yet within my grasp.

Until writing this book, I'd forgotten how I had given up my power to Jenny completely. I had buried my awareness of this dynamic all this time. Had all those therapists tried to tell me? Was I simply unable to hear it until now?

I asked Grace how she could bear hearing my pain all these years.

"She was your daughter. I knew you were forever trying to heal your relationship. But she was always backing you into a corner," she said.

Whenever I would speak to Jenny on the phone, after the first few remarks, Grace could hear my voice rising, knowing that I was trying to defend myself.

"Get off the phone! Now!" she would say.

Knowing that it was going downhill, that the conflict was escalating, she was trying to help me get out. I wanted to close the conversation nicely, but then Jenny would make me wrong for trying to end the call.

"Don't you ever abandon me!" She once said. I caught my breath.

It wasn't a plea for love and connection. It was a threat.

Then came a time a few years later when, once again, I hoped it could be different. She was going to have weight-loss surgery and she seemed so cheerful on the phone, asking me if I would come to spend two days in the hospital with her until a friend arrived who was flying in to help her for the remainder of the first week post-op.

This time Jenny seemed to really want me there. I began to

think that her hopes for having a new life when she lost weight were giving her a lighter mood, a change in her outlook; I could hear that she was looking forward to feeling more attractive and beginning to date again.

She had told me we would have a delicious meal at a lovely restaurant the night before the surgery, saying we could make it a celebration. As we ended the call, we were both feeling upbeat and looking forward to it.

I arrived in Denver in the evening a few weeks later, tired and hungry from spending the day on two planes with no food service. It had been an hour-long ride in from the airport in rush-hour traffic. Jenny seemed exasperated, as if she could hardly be bothered to meet me in the lobby of her apartment building. Or too distracted by something to seem happy to see me.

She began telling me the many different things I needed to know or to do while I was there the next day, and I started writing everything down.

She was irritated. "Why do you keep doing that?"

"Because I'm trying to make sure I don't miss anything!" I explained.

On the way to the restaurant, I could see that she was driving 60 and 70 miles an hour in the city. We were in the outside lane on a one-way street, close to the curb on my side.

"Please slow down," I said. "You're scaring me!"

Jenny just laughed and drove faster. Then I let out a little scream, fearing we were going to run into a van ahead of us at a sudden stop light.

"You're such a drama queen!" she said. She loved scaring me, then mocking me.

We arrived at the restaurant, which was lovely. The menu sounded yummy. I could hardly wait to order. And eat.

"All the entrees sound delicious. I can't decide what to choose! What are your favorites here? What are you going to order to celebrate?" I asked Jenny, trying to jolly her back to remembering her original invitation.

She frowned. "Oh, I can't have anything but water with lemon and a small salad, no dressing. But you go right ahead. Get whatever you want."

Her expression was flat. Matching the conversation. Only because I hadn't had anything since breakfast was I able to eat what must have been a wonderful dinner while she watched me.

Jenny wanted me to spend two nights with her in the hospital on a cot in her room.

"Write this down: how to get to my apartment. You have to drive back there twice each day to feed the cat and make sure she has enough water."

"The cat will be fine if I just go once a day," I said.

"No! I said twice! Just DO IT!" she yelled.

My stomach tightened. Nothing had changed. The combative anger was still at the ready.

I was nervous, driving her Ford Explorer. I had never driven anything so large, sitting so high up. It had been snowing and the streets were icy. Her parking space at the apartment could only be approached by backing in under a low metal awning. I was afraid of damaging something - the car, the awning, or the building. I was also angry. The cat would have been fine with one visit a day, and she knew it. But I didn't want to get into it any further with her, because it was always a no-win conversation. I couldn't find the energy to say "No." and draw even more of her anger.

Later that first day, several hours after the surgery, a nurse came in when Jenny buzzed for help. The nurse was pleasant and sounded very caring, trying to make her more comfortable, but Jenny bit her head off with a demanding tone and demeaning attitude.

"NO! Not like that! You need to fix my sheets! You did that all wrong!" she said.

What a bitch she is, I thought. But I said nothing.

It was dusk and no light had been turned on in the room, which was unusually large for a hospital room. I was quite far away from her bed on my cot, and in the darkening gloom, I couldn't see her face, so I knew she couldn't see mine. I pretended to be napping.

"What?!!" she asked. I said nothing. "WHAT??!!" she demanded.

"Nothing. I didn't say anything." I tried to sound innocent of having just heard her rude remarks. But she was having none of it.

"What were you *thinking* then? You were thinking *something!*"

I wanted to say:

Why are you such a bitch? Why are you so hateful to everyone? Why would you choose to be this kind of person?"

But I just said, "I thought you were rude to that nurse... she was just trying to help you."

"Get out. GET! OUT!!!" she yelled. "I DON'T NEED THIS! I CAN'T STAND THE ENERGY! GET OUT!! GET! OUT!"

When she said it the third time, I picked up my bag and left. I drove back to her apartment and called Grace.

"She told you what to do," she said. "Get out and come home!"

I called Jenny's friend, Elaine, whom I'd known when they both still lived in Dallas. I told her what happened, and that I was going home in the morning. She said she would take over, and check on Jenny at the hospital the next day until her out-of-town friend arrived.

Big as the Whole Wide World

So many years later, while writing this chapter, I came across a folder of emails we'd written to each other long ago. It was shoved all the way to the back of a file drawer. I nearly missed it. It held a multitude of messages back and forth; a barrage of accusations, protests, declarations of love or of newly set boundaries, recriminations, heartfelt apologies, and more... altogether an endless stream of attack and defend, and so sorry/not sorry.

The first one I found was from Jenny. She had written to me a few days later when she came home from the hospital and found that I had flown home. She was stunned that I took her at her word. She thought I should have known that her "Get Out!" speech was meant only about leaving the hospital, and that I'd still be at the apartment to care for her when she got home.

She said she was devastated that I had abandoned her. She told me how much she wanted me there, and how thrilled she had been to see me. She thought we'd been having such a good time at the restaurant the evening before.

We were both filled with such sensitivity, such intensity. Yet we almost never responded with the same energy to a shared experience. We lived in two different worlds. And it seemed it would always break both our hearts.

That was my last visit to Colorado. After her move to California two years later, I tried once again. Grace came with me this time for two days, and since she was there, Jenny was guarded; unpleasant but not combative. The next day Grace had to fly home to meet with clients.

Jenny took Grace to the airport, mentioning that she was flying out for business herself. This was a sudden announcement, but okay. I was relieved she was leaving, sensing a storm brewing with her. And I didn't mind spending my last night in her apartment by myself. I was already planning to fly out the next day for a workshop in LA. I'd get an Uber.

After they left for the airport, I noticed a steamer trunk with an assortment of photos of her friends in small frames arranged together on top of the trunk. Alone at the front of the group was a photo of my mother. I felt my old knee-jerk fear of her surface. I looked away, trying to find a photo of myself. There were none.

On a wall near the trunk there were a few other framed photos. One shows a woman in a winter coat with a wool scarf around her neck, holding her purse. In the background is the Golden Gate Bridge. She's wearing sunglasses. At first, I didn't realize it was a photo of me. And then I got it - she didn't want to look me in the eye. I felt a shiver.

Twenty-Six
Standing Out: New York, Daring to Sing 2003

Meanwhile, those old dreams from the M-G-M musicals never left me.

"In my next life, I'm going to be a singer just like you!" I had said several years earlier to a friend who had just finished a set when she came over to my table at an upscale bar.

"Why don't you do it in *this* life, instead?" Sandy challenged.

"Well," I told her, "Because I only have 3 good notes. I lost my soprano voice during puberty and I never got it back. Then I've been smoking all these years. At office parties, I have to 'lip-sync' Happy Birthday. I don't even have enough range for that! And forget The Star-Spangled Banner."

"I know someone who could get your notes back," she said, "a voice teacher who will work with you. Here's her name. Why don't you just try it?"

Suddenly a huge piece of my childhood dream seemed possible – how incredible was that?

I began to study with this woman who was about my age - nearly 50- a wonderful singer herself, a terrific teacher, and a lot of fun. I began to lose some of my fear of being heard out loud, and she really *was* able to give me back a lot of my lost notes.

But after three months, she said, "There's something wrong. I can't get your voice any higher. Something's in the way and I want you to see this ENT doctor I know. He's the one that visiting stars call if they have vocal problems while they're performing here in Dallas."

I was able to get an appointment quickly and after a rather painful exam, with him peering down my throat into my vocal cords. He told me that I had polyps, and that he wouldn't do the necessary surgery unless I quit smoking for six months.

Nothing else could have ever inspired me to quit smoking all those years. But this did. I found a 12 Step program for smokers, Nicotine Anonymous, and it changed my life. I'm sure it saved it. And it gave me the notes I had been longing for - but had only been able to hear in my head until now. And, bonus! I didn't even have to have the surgery. Quitting cigarettes had allowed my throat to heal by itself.

I went on to take a semester-long class at a local college in musical theatre. And there I was given the name of the best teacher yet - the one who finally taught me proper breathing technique which strengthened my voice even more.

All of this happened several years before I met Grace. Once we were together, we began to go to New York for quick trips to see Broadway shows, and then we discovered individual singers appearing in small clubs. I fell in love with the whole idea of cabaret, where the entertainers sing so many of the "standards," the tunes from the Great American Songbook I had grown up loving and singing in the 40s and 50s, along with wonderful songs from Broadway shows, many of which I already knew and loved, too.

Singing in these small rooms, and sharing stories between songs, created such an intimate connection between the singer and the audience. I was thrilled to discover it. These shows introduced me to new songs too, and I began to expand my repertoire.

Around this time, I began rehearsing every week with Bobby Barber, a wonderfully soulful jazz pianist and such a dear man. With a surprise inheritance from my uncle, I found the courage to take us into a professional studio to record two CDs, one with us together and a solo one for Bobby. He played like a dream, always - and he seemed as if recording was second nature to him, while I was so intimidated with the process, embarrassed at being the amateur I was. But beyond the intimidation, my passion for doing this for both of us was greater than my shyness. I'm still grateful to that frightened me of twenty years ago that I had the guts to do it. I couldn't believe my life!

One Sunday afternoon I was on my own in New York; Grace couldn't get away for this trip. I went to an open mic at a small French restaurant in the Theatre District one Sunday afternoon, where the woman who hosted it introduced herself as Trudi and invited me to sing. At first, I demurred, but then she asked me a third time.

"If you'll sing and the owners like you, they'll give you a show of your own here." Well!

I had to say yes.

When I got up to sing, I stood near the drummer while I waited for another singer to finish his song. I was terrified as I waited, a nervous wreck with cottonmouth. I looked at the wall behind the drummer where I saw a painting of a trio and a singer. Painting was what I'd spent my whole adult life doing instead of singing, which I really wanted to be doing more than anything.

You can just sit down now and go back home and paint a picture of a singer, or you can stay here and just sing from your heart right now, and see what happens. Can you let yourself have this moment you've always dreamed of? There it was again: The old theme: *should I go?*

should I stay?

I stayed. I sang. I got the show! It was on the books for April 3rd.

Giving myself permission to open my heart this way was so freeing that my fear melted away into pure joy.

An hour later, waiting outside the theater before going in to watch Elaine Stritch's one-woman tour de force *Elaine Stritch At Liberty*, I was squealing with astonishment on my cellphone to Grace, "I got the show!! I'm really coming back to New York to have MY OWN SHOW!!" Grace was thrilled for me!

The other people who were standing there, also waiting to enter the theatre, were cheering me, too. "Congratulations!!" "Good for you!!" "That's awesome!!"

I got to my seat, the orchestra opened with a gorgeous flourish, and out walked Elaine Stritch. I said to myself, *this is the most New York night of my life!* And I have lived another 23 years since then to report that nothing, and no one else's performance since has knocked me out like hers that night. Maybe it was because for those two hours, I knew that I had a show coming up too, and I felt like a New York cabaret performer, my own self.

I flew back to New York for my show a few months later and had exactly one day to rehearse with a fabulous pianist that a friend had found for me. Tracy Stark was and still is a godsend for everyone she plays for. A genius at making me feel like I deserved to be there. At the time, I had no idea she played for people all over the New York cabaret scene and was known and loved for her own original shows as a composer and performer. She even tours as music director for two famous singers. For that rehearsal day and the performance on the following night, she was there just to help me shine. And I did.

Finally, I beat the odds. Finally, I had an incredible win in New York. Thank you, God. How does it get any more wonderful than this?

Twenty-Seven
LOSING OUT: Gone 2003-2005

Grace and I had three wonderful years together before the bottom fell out of my freelance art career. In addition to our further life coach training with Debbie Ford, we were joining her on workshop cruises in the Caribbean and the Mediterranean. This was all very new for Grace, and I loved watching her enjoyment, exploring foreign places she'd never thought of visiting. We even traveled on our own to Paris, twice. And we had such a great time together.

We respected each other's spiritual beliefs; we shared the same political views. We laughed together, with our usually identical senses of humor. But our compatibility began to suffer when my freelance career ended abruptly, and I suddenly had no income.

One day my only remaining client, like the rest of them I had once depended upon, told me they too had hired an in-house staff working on computers. They'd be turning out electronically the work I had drawn by hand for years and had taken for granted would always be there for me.

Here I'd left my job as an ad agency art director to do this specialized type of freelance work, drawing storyboard frames for TV commercials just because there was so much money in it, even though I was told that it would burn me out in a year. I'd been at it for sixteen years by this time. Sixteen years of mostly all-nighters, with my eyes burning and my lungs filling with the fumes from the benzine markers, mixing with the smoke from all the cigarettes I'd been smoking.

Even as I was stunned at the news, I was so exhausted from constantly grinding out this work that I must admit, my first instinct was to be grateful. An overwhelming weight had been lifted off me, through no fault of my own, I thought.

Only for a moment was I relieved, however, as it immediately began to change the dynamic between us. Once again, I had no money. And Grace, not one who liked discussing her feelings, left me to myself to figure out what I was going to do next.

I had always made my living solely as an artist and I had always made good money. With such vibrant health and high energy, I felt that surely there would always be another vehicle for my talents that would pay me well. Even after my ill-conceived pitch for the New York fashion account sent me into a bankruptcy that took five years to pay off, I still wasn't motivated to save anything. And after all the times in my career that I had come to this point, I certainly should have learned by now to set aside something for another "what if."

But instead, true to my magical thinking, I always believed that the work was there for my asking, and I had continued spending every cent I made. It was such an innate part of me, that I didn't even pause to think of living otherwise.

By now I had to admit that this was a reaction to my mother's idea that I should be saving my money for the eventual "rainy day" she told me to expect. I thought that was something she believed just because she had lived through the Depression.

When I was growing up, I remember when my father brought home a shiny new car. Under her breath, she remarked: "We're going to the poorhouse!" I had thought it was just a figure of speech. Many years later in the family tree I created with online genealogy, I found that my mother had an Uncle Tolley who did actually live and die in a poorhouse in Michigan.

He was a *prisoner* there!

How tragic, and how I wished she had told me this sad story. My entire attitude toward making money and saving it might have been turned upside down, and I might never have set myself up to keep winding up with nothing, as I kept finding myself. On the other hand, perhaps it would have stifled my sense of adventure, and my belief in myself.

At that point, the dynamic in our relationship shifted so sharply that I would have left Grace if I could have, because she clearly was not happy supporting us without my help.

※

That year her mother died. We moved into her spacious home which Grace inherited in a tiny town 45 minutes away from Dallas, the city I loved, and the only place where I could imagine finding new work of some sort as a freelance artist.

When I was unable to turn up anything, as computers began to dominate everywhere at ad agencies, I found a job coaching women at a weight loss clinic, driving back into Dallas each day. The difference in my income was shocking. And it was painful to admit how little respect, or really, how little understanding of money I'd had all these years.

I had just become eligible for taking early Social Security payments and so I jumped at the chance. That helped, but only for my personal needs, not enough for me to contribute very much to the household expenses.

Over the next few years Grace and I became more and more distant. Even though I felt she no longer enjoyed my company, she was too kind to ask me to leave.

A lifetime of not knowing myself, of not understanding the dynamics of survival, learning skills like saving money as my mother had warned, and as sensible people do, had finally brought me down. I moved to the guest bedroom, which seemed appropriate, since by now I felt like a guest who had stayed too long but was allowed to remain out of pity, simply because she had nowhere else to go.

Twenty-Eight
Time Out: The Camino de Santiago 2012

I felt rotten. Embarrassed and ashamed to once again be caught unaware of the reality of money and life. I knew Grace was unhappy too, but she didn't talk about it. She immersed herself in the elder-care legal work that she loved. And when she decided she also wanted to become a minister, she enrolled at a seminary within a nearby university, and poured the rest of her energy and her focus into that, all while keeping her law practice going. We didn't talk much.

Life went on, though my heart wasn't in it.

Jenny became successful in her work and even more beautiful, having lost the weight she wanted to, and began dating again. Soon she fell in love and seemed very happy, living with a man whose career was in the same IT field. She invited me to come for a visit to meet him, saying then we could go on a little weekend trip together, just the two of us.

When I arrived and met him, I thought he seemed very nice and like a quiet, responsible type. I wondered how he felt about her intense personality; maybe it was exciting for him. At least her attention had been less focused on me. Since she'd met him, our phone calls were much more pleasant.

Although we were still cautious with each other, we were able to get through our weekend jaunt with our mutually favorite pastime, going to the movies. That was where we'd always had such fun, gobbling popcorn, exchanging knowing looks when we reacted to something that was happening on the screen at the same instant. I had missed those times.

I left my job at the weight-loss clinic and began working parttime at a large hospital in the city, taking photos of newborn babies and though it paid little, I loved it. I continued to read Numerology charts whenever I had a referral. And I was hoping to build a life-coaching clientele, but this was before social media had become a means of marketing one's business, and my clients were few. My life-coaching offering was to be completed in a 3-month time frame, so there was the need to keep looking for new clients who were ready to do deep inner work.

I was unable to move away, but one day I felt I just had to get away. I looked online and found I had enough frequent flyer miles for a trip, so I flew off to see my friend Katie in Cambridge for a few days. It was such a relief to spend time with someone who was happy to see me, to laugh again in easy conversation. She took me to interesting little cafes with exotic foreign food, and we rode on the MTA to the Boston Museum of Art, where I was excited to see they had many of the most famous paintings by my favorite artist, John Singer Sargent.

The day before flying home I phoned Tink, another friend who lives in Cambridge. I had met Tink at that singing workshop in Italy sixteen years earlier and we had stayed in touch all this time. She was delighted to hear from me and invited Katie and me to come by for lunch on our way to the airport the next day.

"I'm so glad you're here this week and not last week or the week before," Tink said. "I wouldn't have answered the phone then, and I would have missed the chance to see you!"

"Why not?" I said, afraid something dreadful might have happened in her family.

She said she had just returned from another pilgrimage, the walk across Spain on the Camino de Santiago, and she didn't want to disturb the peace it had brought her, by getting back into the flow of normal life just yet. I was surprised that any trip could stop time that profoundly.

At our lunch the next day, I told her how it touched me that the Camino had affected her so deeply. Did she have any pictures of her trip? Her laptop was nearby and when she opened it a photo filled the screen of a lush forest with immensely tall trees, darkly green, and a soft dirt path that was winding into the forest and out of sight. In that instant, I felt my soul walk into that scene, and it didn't come out until I returned home after walking the Camino myself a year later. I was instantly and completely committed to this pilgrimage.

I came home from Cambridge in a wholly different mindset. Positive and rejuvenated. This was a feeling I'd never had - being called to commit to something without having any idea why.

It was exciting to me that it gave me a focus I didn't question. Fortunately, there was a definitive online roadmap. Tink sent me to a Facebook group, American Pilgrims on The Camino, that was filled with posts by others who were also preparing for the Camino, or who had already been there, and were overflowing with enormous amounts of information on how to get ready for this adventure.

This was such a new experience. For openers, I had never been athletic, nor wanted to be. I had been such an indoor child growing up, reading books, drawing and coloring, with almost no connection to nature at all except for those two weeks at the lake in Michigan each summer as a child. And I was almost 75 years old. A little late for this? Not at all according to my online source. There were plenty of people my age and older hiking the Camino.

For nearly a year I trained in parks or at the gym, and I had to get equipment. I field-tested and returned several pairs of boots and shoes and walked around the REI store trying out an assortment of backpacks loaded with weights so I could decide which was the most comfortable. I pored over the online advice from people who were there now, from those who had been there, and from those who were getting ready, like I was; even from some who were going back for the fifth time.

A month before I left, I read a post from a woman who had just begun the Camino a few days earlier.

"Thank heavens I trained on the elliptical!" she said.

The Elliptical? Holy Cow, I thought. Well, I guess I'd better do it. The first time: 13 seconds, and I thought *no way*. But I kept it up until I could do 60 minutes at a time, at least 4 times a week for the next month until I left home on September 1st.

Grace seemed to like the fact that I was working on *something*. The energy between us was a little warmer, and as I got stronger in my training and she realized I might really make this happen, I felt that she respected what I was doing, even if I didn't have a clear sense of why I was doing it. She honored my calling.

I told her that I wasn't sure why I was so driven to go, but that maybe I was meant to meet someone over there (and then be out of her hair). I had read that a lot of people meet a Someone on the Camino to spend the rest of their lives with. I still felt attractive, and I was healthy for my age, though I was certainly no prize in the financial department.

Still the girl in love with Hollywood endings, I had hope in my heart that there could still be something wonderful ahead for my life; that it might yet be possible. And I thought that Grace would certainly feel some relief if I were no longer financially dependent on her.

The day before I left, she gave me a heartfelt card. It reminded me of how we had always loved exchanging cards in earlier, happier days. The printed message sounded like she might possibly be afraid of losing me. *Oh.* Or was it Goodbye?

I flew back to Boston because there was a direct flight there leaving for Paris, and I spent the night with Katie again before I made the big leap. She and her husband Dennis had just moved the day before, so I slept on the floor on an air mattress, surrounded by cartons. It was so dear to have her wave me goodbye for the trip that began in my heart the last time we were together, only a year before.

I felt so free, not knowing why I was going, nor how it might change my life. I just trusted that because I felt so guided, it must be in Divine Order. Maybe, instead of meeting someone, I would return home with new inspired ideas for my work in the world. And the ability to support myself again. It could change everything if I could become financially responsible, at last.

Arriving in Paris again was thrilling. I always imagine each time that I might have lived there in a past life. And I was looking forward to revisiting the places I'd already been in this life. I had booked a car to pick me up at Charles de Gaulle airport instead of taking the train into the city since I had my backpack and a large duffel bag to maneuver.

Coming through the same tunnel where Princess Diana had died was chilling. But on the other side, familiar sights returned, and I was so grateful to be back. There are other ways to approach the Camino; many people fly into Madrid, or Barcelona. But Paris means so much more to me! And very soon I arrived at the tiny plaza surrounding the Pantheon, to the small hotel on the Left Bank where Grace and I had stayed on wonderful visits several years before. I love the neighborhood and after checking in, and leaving my bags in my room, I left to see if the boulangerie with the perfect eclairs and the Tibetan restaurant we had loved were still there. I made my way around the corner and there they were, right where I remembered them. And then I was sad that she wasn't here with me to enjoy them again.

I had decided to give myself two days and nights to get adjusted to the time zone change before I took the train to the French border with Spain, where the most popular path to the Camino begins.

Before I left home, I had made arrangements to meet someone from my wonderful go-to source, American Pilgrims on the Camino, on my second night in Paris. He was a middle-aged American man who was also about to begin the pilgrimage on the Camino, and he seemed nice enough online. He took the Metro across town from where he was staying at a hostel and met me at a restaurant in my Paris neighborhood. He paid for my glass of wine, and we chatted about our upcoming adventure. Then I suggested we try the Tibetan restaurant for dinner. I wasn't expecting to pay for his meal, although at the end of it, it became apparent that he did; after all, he explained, he'd paid for my wine. He hadn't been to Paris before and asked if I had any ideas about where to go next.

At this point it would have been prudent for me to have returned to my hotel around the corner, but I really did want to see a nighttime outdoor exhibit of sculptures in the Gardens at the Rodin Museum. I'd never been there before and wasn't sure where it was located, so we got a taxi which I was happy to pay for, not wanting to try the Metro. It was a beautiful exhibit, but the night was pitch black, and the floodlights were few and far between. When we decided to leave, I realized that this was not on a street where taxis would be continually driving by.

A guard pointed down to a major street at the corner before he closed and locked the gate to the Rodin Gardens.

As we walked down to the cross street, I could see that it was a large thoroughfare, so I expected it to be dotted with shops and restaurants and hotels. But no. The street was wide, but with no traffic. The buildings were large but all of them were dark. Looking at a map now, I can see that one of them was the Swedish Embassy. This was strictly a daytime business neighborhood.

We walked for a few blocks, and I kept hoping for a taxi, praying that we would soon come to some lighted places with activity. The night was so dark, the streetlights were far between and I was getting nervous. Blocks earlier, we had passed a bus stop and now this fellow decided he was going to go back there to wait for a bus to return to his hostel. *Are you kidding??*

"Don't leave me here alone, for God's sake!" I pleaded.

I prayed even *harder* for a taxi. How could a gentleman abandon me to walk alone in the dark in a foreign city? But more to the point now: how could I have been so careless to have continued the evening with him?

And then *thank God* a taxi appeared out of nowhere. I swear I didn't even see it coming down the street. It was just suddenly here. I left him heading in the other direction toward the bus stop, since he didn't want to pay for the part of the taxi ride that would have been his.

The next morning: *Well, this is it, kid!* The first day of the Camino. The hotel agreed to hold onto my duffel bag for a month. I tossed my backpack over my shoulders and jumped into a taxi headed for the railway station. I doubt that it was as effortless as I just made that sound; I was 74 years old. But I felt young and strong, and I was in, and we were off!

When I arrived at the station, the board announcing all the trains was the largest I'd ever seen. I bought a ticket for Saint-Jean-Pied-de-Port, the town at the border of France and Spain, where I would be taking my first steps on the Camino. While I waited there was no place to sit down. Walking was more comfortable than standing still with the pack on my back, so I paced up and down the vast area, which accessed so many tracks, hoping I would board the correct train. Also pacing the area were two very muscled and serious-looking French soldiers in uniform carrying assault rifles at the ready in both hands. Their eyes were constantly moving across the crowd, as if they were expecting danger to erupt at any second.

I was alert too, but finally able to relax when I confirmed that I was on the right train for sure.

Oooofff!! How incredible! Now I was really on my way! When I changed trains in Biarritz, I was going to connect with Anette, a coaching client of mine from Germany. I had known her only from our Skype sessions until now.

Anette was a veteran of two Caminos; one she had hiked and one in which she traveled the entire 500 miles on a bicycle through the incredibly high Pyrenees mountains that greet one at the very beginning of exiting Saint Jean. She told me she would already be on the train I was going to transfer to, and the minute I heard her call my name I relaxed completely, knowing I was in good hands.

Well, now we've caught up to where I was at the beginning of this book, and now you know why I told you that my relationship was disintegrating, and that I had no idea why I had come to walk the Camino.

After an hour or so, we arrived at Saint-Jean and disembarked with our backpacks onto a very old and bumpy cobbled platform. Anette led me to the street behind the train station, where we immediately faced more cobblestones on a very vertical climb leading up to the hostel where we would spend the night. Tall, slender, fit and twenty years younger than I, she was way ahead of me from the start. Wow! We were already high in the mountains, and I was gasping for air.

She glanced back at me, saw my struggle, and quickly and easily grabbed my backpack and kept going without breaking her stride.

When we arrived on level ground, we went to a building that gave out the Pilgrim Passports, which would allow us to stay in hostels (*albergues* in Spanish) for very little money and to eat cheaply but well at the restaurants and cafes along the way.

Before leaving home, both Anette and I had made reservations at an albergue here run by Dutch women. Leaving the passport office, we arrived just in time for a delicious supper, meeting friendly women and men of different ages and nationalities. We were all bubbling with excitement about the adventure we were about to begin, but soon after we ate, we retired to our bunk beds so we could all get an early start in the morning. Night owl that I am, and so excited to be here at last, I couldn't relax enough to get much sleep.

I'd read that the first and second day after leaving Saint Jean hold the steepest, most difficult climb of the entire 500 miles. I woke up happy and excited, and already dressed. I had slept in my clothes, as I had already read this is what everyone does on the Camino. I grabbed my pack, and when I arrived downstairs for breakfast, I heard that some people had already left even earlier. Others were taking things out of their packs to lighten them. There was a basket of discarded items there for anyone who wanted them.

Anette looked at me, and from her very direct German gaze, I knew something had changed.

"You can't go with me", she said. "You're not in good enough shape to do the first two days in these mountains. You'll have to find a taxi to take you down to the base of the mountain and begin at Roncesvalles."

Her judgment of my condition was so unexpected. I careened from embarrassment (*not in good enough shape? I suddenly felt flabby and toad-like*) to fear (*I thought Anette would show me 'the ropes' and now I will be alone!*) to anger (*How could you do that to me after all I've done for you as your coach?*) to arrogance (*I would never walk out on you like that!*) to judgment (*How rude! Europeans are so blunt!*) to gratitude (*Oh! She is probably saving me from a terrible danger!*) Thank you, Anette.

Showing no emotion at all, and without waiting for my response, Anette grabbed her pack and walking sticks, turned and left.

Twenty-Nine
MORE TIME OUT: Pilgrimage 2013

I found my way back to the Pilgrim passport office to ask for help in getting a taxi that would take me down the mountain to the town of Roncevalles. I waited for what seemed like a very long time, making me wonder if they were coming at all (Paris redux.) But at last, a taxi-van pulled up, and I squeezed in with others already inside.

We began a steep 45-minute descent all the way down to the flat and safe entrance to the Camino, the much easier beginning of the entire 500 miles. Anette had taken the toughest route to get to this spot where I was now standing. I was thankful that she was already a veteran of the Camino and had seen right away that I was not fit enough to attempt it. What had been an easy drive down the mountain in under an hour would take a skilled climber a day or more to descend.

A sign announcing the distance 800 kilometers (500 miles)

was right there where the taxi-van let me out at the entrance, a dirt path leading immediately into a beautiful forest. I wondered if it was the same forest I had first seen on Tink's laptop, the image that my Soul had entered one year ago, to the day.

I hopped out of the little van, got my pack slung onto my back and carried my walking sticks in my hands. The beauty all around me was simply glorious. I wanted to just stand there for a while, taking it all in, but instead I took a deep breath and walked into the forest, wondering what to do with my sticks, the one piece of equipment I forgot to test. I could see there were people in the distance ahead, but they were too far away for me to see their sticks and how they were using them. I turned around and saw a young, quite overweight woman behind me, whose pack was lumpy and enormous. It looked like it would soon overpower her.

"Do you know how to use these sticks?" I asked.

"I have no idea. I don't have any," she said.

I was pretty sure we were going to need them, so I loaned her one of mine and we began walking and talking, using our solo sticks like canes. I began to feel very fit next to her—even if I was more than old enough to be her grandmother.

Victoria and I walked together without seeing any other pilgrims for nearly three hours on a winding but still flat dirt path. And then we began to feel raindrops. We stopped to pull our rain ponchos out of our bags, but they were ineffectual when the wind began whipping up too, blowing them over our heads. Suddenly it became a real storm. The rain began pouring down heavily and thunder boomed loudly as lightning struck on all sides - so close we could hear it even though we couldn't see it. I'd always heard that you shouldn't stand under a tree in a storm, or you could be hit by lightning, and here we were in the middle of nothing but trees, with no end in sight.

In this part of the forest someone had put down large pieces of flagstone onto the path, the kind you'd see on a patio floor or on a garden path. With all this rain, they were very slippery. Suddenly I was sitting down on one, before even realizing that I was falling. Thankfully, it didn't hurt at all, and as Victoria was young and strong, she was able to give me a hand and pull me to an upright position.

We walked for another hour or more in the pouring rain and we were drenched. And cold. Our ponchos were meant for showers, not storms. The thunder and lightning had continued without letup. It was quite a frightening introduction to my adventure.

For all that time that we were walking, there had been no sign of a road. And then suddenly the forest came to an abrupt end, and we were standing on a road at last. All at once, the rain and thunder and lightning ended too.

By now, it was getting dark. We soon entered a tiny village not far down the road and found our way to an albergue where, *thanks be to the Highest*, they had a room! And we had arrived in time for dinner, maybe the best meal I'd ever yet had.

Our clothes were soaked, and on the Camino, you can only carry one change of clothing, because of the weight and the space more items would take up in your pack. Though I did begin to suspect that Victoria had brought an extended wardrobe. We were very lucky that this albergue had an electric dryer so we would be able to dry our clothes, but I was concerned that my leather boots couldn't possibly get dry by morning. I learned something that night when the host rolled up newspapers and stuffed them in my boots. By morning they were very damp, but bearable.

This began a daily, often hourly exercise in gratitude. I was also incredibly thankful to have had Victoria's company that day. I shuddered again to imagine how much more frightened I would have been in that storm alone. I'm not sure I could have even regained my footing and gotten up from those slippery flagstones by myself.

After dinner that night, when we went to our room, I opened my guidebook and read that the forest we'd finally emerged from was the same one where the witches had lived who were executed during the Spanish Inquisition. I'd always felt that they had not been witches at all, but really medicine women, or midwives, working with herbs and helping other women with comfort and words of wisdom. Still, there *was* all that thunder and lightning. Were we being chased out of their forest? I know, I've seen too many movies.

The next day after breakfast Victoria and I headed out on the trail along with many others making our way down the mountain to Zubiri. But we didn't try to keep up with anyone;

between my age and Victoria's weight and the size of her pack, we were about even in our walking speed. I had no idea we'd been walking uphill during all those hours in the thunderstorm in the forest, but we must have arrived atop another mountain because the road to Zubiri was a very steep descent. And like much of the Camino path, it was rutted with large gnarly tree roots, deep crevasses and rocks that ranged in size from very large gravel to boulders strewn along the sides of the path. The walking sticks were indispensable to keep balance, and I wished I had both of mine.

I heard someone sobbing loudly and turned to see two young men holding up a young woman, one on either side, who had evidently injured her knees. Mascara was running down her pretty face. She wasn't crying as much as whining and swearing. Near me, two older women were walking together and one remarked that the young woman was her daughter who wanted to come along to the Camino but hadn't wanted to do any of the necessary training to get in shape for it. I wondered if she would take the next plane home or stay with it; and if it would eventually transform her, as the Camino is said to do.

We arrived in Zubiri and there were no spaces available at any albergues at all. We went to a meeting place for pilgrims and were told that there were no places to stay in the next two towns either because of a local festival. So, Victoria and I went into a dark bar and called for a taxi. When he finally arrived, the driver took us on a long and expensive ride all the way into Pamplona, a major city that holds the annual running of the bulls, made famous by Ernest Hemingway in his book *The Sun Also Rises*. Since we had no idea where to go, the driver chose a hotel for us and dropped us off.

Victoria and I had dinner in the hotel restaurant and this time we were able to book separate rooms. When she wasn't at breakfast the next morning, I went to the desk to call her room. They said she had already checked out hours earlier. Thankfully, she'd left my walking stick for me.

This was the day my Camino truly began. After I got over the surprising sting of Victoria's secret exit, I soon found I loved being completely on my own.

After making my way so carefully among the boulders hour after hour on that tense descent into Zubiri, I decided to stop carrying my pack. Instead, I had it carted from village to village in little mini-vans for a small fee. Unencumbered by the weight of the pack, I was more surefooted. I felt perfectly capable of taking care of myself, and now that I had both of my walking sticks, I knew I'd be able to navigate the challenging terrain. My wonderful guidebook explained how and where to ask for help if I needed it.

From then on, I felt as free as a 12-year-old girl without a care in the world; no schedule, no appointments to keep, no one else to take care of and nothing to do at last but feel this new joy of being surrounded and immersed in Nature. There had been nothing before in my life to compare with this feeling of having myself all to myself. For nearly four weeks, it was a continual open-eyed meditation. And in the midst of such ravishing beauty.

I have never felt more loved by God. Never more secure or more certain that I was safe and was exactly where and who I was meant to be.

In sending my pack on ahead, I had to refer to my guidebook listing all the albergues and choose one each morning for my destination. The available amenities at each place were varied, but the most important thing was to make sure there was internet service so I could keep Grace alert to my continued safety. Even though I had no idea what would become of our relationship when I returned, I knew that she was concerned for my safety, and that made me feel safer. I was so glad to hear her voice once we were connected on our international iPhones.

Most of the albergues had washing machines but I never again found an electric dryer. I learned that the first thing to do when I arrived was to change to my only other clothing and wash what I'd been wearing. Then I'd hang the pieces on the clothesline and hope they would all be dry by morning so I could put them in my pack before sending it off in the minivan to the next albergue. We slept in our clean clothes, so we were up and ready to leave at first light in the morning. First Light is practically pitch-dark, but after you've been walking for just a little while and are ready to find breakfast at a cafe, the sun is shining. Occasionally one of the albergues will serve breakfast before you leave, which is lovely.

At the end of my first week, I spent the night in Viana at an albergue that had triple-stacked bunk beds, instead of double, and I was fortunate to find one of the lowest bunks. It was a large municipal albergue, not a lovely private one, as I would have preferred. But then I was just learning to read the symbols in my guidebook that would tell me the difference.

There were over a hundred of us spending the night there, with only one rest room for the women and another for the men. They didn't serve dinner or breakfast, and as in most alberques, the curfew was ten p.m. We found ourselves in the middle of a big celebration happening in the village that night where we were having dinner, but we didn't stay as we had to be back before the doors were locked at ten.

At midnight, someone opened the door to our room that held at least fifty of us, and snapping on the light, asked if there was a doctor who could come quickly to help! A young man from Australia had stayed out to join the celebration way past the curfew and had tried to climb the three-story wall of the building to crawl in through a window. In his drunken state, he'd lost his grip and had fallen to the street. He was carried inside, and an ambulance came to take him away to a hospital. When we came downstairs the next morning, there were still traces of blood on the foyer floor.

Before I left that morning, the man who'd slept on the bunk above me asked how long I had been traveling and when my departure flight was scheduled. When I gave him that information, I told him I had been walking for a week already.

"Well, you're never going to make it to Santiago then, unless you take some shortcuts!" he said, and happily set to work for an hour, referring to a guidebook and then drawing a map showing me where I could take a bus or a train at different points along the route, so I could make it to Santiago before I had to fly out.

Getting to Santiago where the bones of the disciple St. James rest, and claiming the prized certificate, the Compostela, which proved you had completed the Camino, were considered the most important goals. Since he had hiked the Camino before, he wanted to help me reach it. With this map he felt he could spare me the roughest parts, especially the long stretches of the Meseta, a flat area with virtually no trees offering protection from the Sun. I was so thankful for his effort and followed it to the letter, taking one bus and one train ride between major cities. Still, I felt like I was cheating as I sat in comfort, watching through the window as other pilgrims left each city to get back on the path.

Before leaving home, I had created a private Facebook page "Sherle On The Camino" where I posted daily photos, videos and notes for my friends to follow my adventure. Looking at it now ten years later puts me right back there on the rugged path. The memories flash back all the time and I'm there, not only for the grand moments but for the tiny ones too, looking for the painted yellow arrows that guided me; sometimes painted on pavement or on grass along the road, sometimes on the sides of old buildings in the villages.

Every evening after dinner a Pilgrim mass was held at churches both large and small, depending on the size of the village or town I was in, to bless us on our way. We were sometimes even given front row seats. It was such a sweet feeling to be blessed by the local villagers everywhere we went.

On one day that was particularly hot, the road to the albergue I'd chosen was long and arduous. The sun was intense and there were no trees for quite a stretch. As I walked alone that day, two young Irish girls passed me. One of them called out a "Hello! Buen Camino!" the greeting we all exchanged all along the way. She handed me a bunch of grapes as they passed. What a wonderful gift! They quenched my thirst and I was thankful that I didn't have to stop to get my water bottle out of my daypack.

A while later I came upon them again, speaking with an older couple, all of them standing under the shade of a small lone tree, talking about how much they all loved Leonard Cohen. I stopped and opened my phone to a YouTube recording of his song "Dance Me to The End Of Love" and we all sang along together.

At another albergue in Astorga the following week, all of us pilgrims were cooking a meal together and one woman brought out her ukulele. We all began singing Leonard Cohen's "Hallelujah." His music was the most perfect accompaniment for the Camino. You could feel how it joined the hearts of everyone who loved it.

My most favorite stay by far was at a wonderful small albergue that I found in Burgos. Run by a French woman, Marie-Noelle, it slept only twenty people. It was fitted-out in a very sleek and updated style, with large, beautiful stainless-steel bathrooms with lovely light and wonderful showers; quite a surprise since it occupied the upper floor in the back of a very old, now renovated, church. The beds were the most comfortable I'd found and of course the food was delicious.

After dinner Marie-Noelle handed a small book to each of us, written in our respective languages. It was the story of the road to Emmaus. She asked us to read it and then to select one sentence that meant the most to us, to be read aloud to the group, who were all from several different countries. What a touching request. The following morning, she woke us by playing a recording of a choir singing. They sounded like angels. She began it so softly I barely stirred from sleep and then it so gradually became louder until I was gently and fully awakened. I wish I had it now to play me to sleep at night and to wake me each day.

The benefit of being older and slower than most others on the path is that I was usually alone during the morning on my walk. This gave me privacy and the privilege of being able to cry and pray and scream and sing to myself as much as I wanted or needed to. I prayed out loud with only the mountains and the skies, the trees, the rocks along the way or the soft forest path - and God and the Angels - to hear me.

As I walked on, I thought about those first three years with Grace, when I had felt so sure that we truly loved each other and that we would be together for the rest of our lives. While I was earning money, everything was loving and kind, easy and fun. It seemed a miracle that we had met in the first place, and though I never imagined it ending, I never took us for granted either. I loved her soul. Now I felt she was lost to me. I kept moving along the path, one foot and then the other.

I asked for forgiveness, and I gave forgiveness to all those who had hurt me, betrayed me, and had in any way stopped loving me. I thought about Jack and Chris and Ted. I knew they had all suffered as children, as I had, in ways that had made them the men they became. When I first met Jack, he had told me in a rare moment of vulnerability, about a horribly wounding experience he'd had with his first-grade teacher. It explained so much to me about how he had chosen to operate in the world. Chris had been so shamed by his father, who humiliated him constantly as a child, and he'd been sexually abused during high school by the man who owned the pharmacy where he had worked at the soda fountain. Ted had been made to feel less than his sister by his authoritarian father, and I know he was always feeling that he had to measure up as president of the family business. He might have preferred another career.

I saw beyond my own pain. I knew we had all suffered. And as I forgave these men, crying loudly into the beauty of this precious world all around me, something deep within me was releasing.

A week after my return from the Camino, I had a phone call from his widow telling me Ted had died, that he had asked her to let me know.

I flashed back to the last time I had seen him, nearly ten years earlier. I was back in Indianapolis, to visit an old friend and spontaneously decided to call him to ask if he would drive me to the airport, the same one he had taken me to when I was only 26, heartbroken over Christopher, and heading to Miami, when we had flirted all the way there. I was surprised when he said yes. Maybe he was processing old issues himself. Or maybe he was just curious to see how I'd aged. By that time, I was in my sixties, and he was nearly ten years older.

When he arrived to pick me up, all that time collapsed, and all those old feelings rushed back.

He arrived early and we had plenty of time to get to the airport, so he suggested we stop for lunch on the way. There was no one anywhere near our table in the middle of the afternoon, so I decided to share my heart, telling him that I had never stopped loving him. Despite his betrayal.

"It was never the same with anyone else like it was with us," he offered.

I knew he felt he was handing me a rose with that line, but I wanted to scream.

"Then why did you betray me like that?? Why wasn't I enough? How could you let me go? I asked.

He didn't, couldn't answer. Tears were rolling down my face into my soup. He tried to make a little joke. "The waitress will think you don't like your food," he said. I hadn't touched it.

We continued the drive to the airport, talking in the car. He told me he had cancer. When we reached the airport and he parked the car, he kissed me, then told me he couldn't say more because he was married now. Again. I imagine she must have figured him out and put her foot down, or maybe he was being 'faithful' now because he was old, and he'd let go of the chase.

I got out of the car, walked up the steps to the entrance. At the top I turned around and saw that Ted was standing by the car door, watching me leave before getting in. Once I was inside the building I ran into an empty restroom, sat down on a toilet, and sobbed without caring who heard, until there was nothing left.

Then I went to the gate and boarded the plane to come gratefully home to my darling Grace.

Big as the Whole Wide World

When his widow called telling me he was gone, I had no more tears. Now I thanked him for the good times, for those six years of lunchtime trysts, when I was young and so in love, feeling gloriously alive and utterly fulfilled.

All along the Camino I kept up my endless questioning of my relationship with Jenny and why we had been unhappy with each other for such a long time. I cried, I prayed, I forgave her, and I asked for her forgiveness. I felt that it must have been something I'd done, or failed to do, that earned her wrath, though I never knew what she held against me, and she would never say. This was a pain far worse than either divorce. I had met those men when I was an adult. But I had given birth to her. And we had once loved each other with such innocent hearts. No matter how much I longed to return to that love, it seemed to mean nothing to her.

Finally, I saw that I didn't come to the Camino to meet a Someone. I came to let go of what was no longer mine.

It is set up that pilgrims who only hike the last hundred kilometers are eligible for the prized Compostela, so many people will walk only that portion. When I finally arrived at that jumping off spot where the last hundred kilometers began, the energy changed. The simplicity and quiet of seeing only a few people on the path each day were gone. As much as I had loved my solitary walks and my time alone with my thoughts and tears and prayers, my inner work felt complete for now.

This last week on the path I met a lovely Swedish family: two sisters in their sixties, Agneta and Gunilla and Gunilla's 30-year-old son, Andreas. They were only able to take the time to walk those last hundred kilometers, and they hadn't had a guidebook to bring along. As I shared my experiences at dinner, we all enjoyed each other so much that we decided to spend that last week together. Now I was glad to have their company and I looked forward to sharing the powerful culmination of our journey at the Cathedral of St. James in Santiago.

We laughed so much along the way that week, even when we were awash, walking all one afternoon in a downpour, the only one I'd been in since that first day leaving Roncesvalles. We were lucky to find comfortable alberques with private rooms and baths each night that week; what a luxury after all the bunkbeds and bathrooms shared with many.

Walking on a highway overpass we entered the city of Santiago and exhaled. But there was another five miles to go before entering the ancient part of the city to find the Cathedral of St. James. When we reached that final destination, we were greeted with a bagpiper playing under an arch that signaled the entrance to the original medieval town.

We went first to the immense Cathedral to pay our respects to the Apostle St. James, thanking him for our safety on our pilgrimage, and I prayed for his blessing on Grace's upcoming confirmation at the seminary. I felt her presence with me and knew the blessing was bestowed. Then we were off to the Pilgrim office to get our Compostela.

We arrived early the next day at the enormous cathedral to get good seats up close for the Pilgrim's Mass at noon, where they swing the Botafumeiro, which I'd read in the guidebook is the largest censer in the world for spreading the incense smoke, weighing 175 pounds and measuring five feet in height. As choral voices filled the air, the Botafumeiro was pulled with thick ropes by eight priests, swinging back and forth from a pulley system high above the altar, reaching speeds of 80 kilometers per hour. It's quite an astounding spectacle. All at once a fitting climax and a humbling tribute to honor our extraordinary efforts to arrive here at last.

Walking this legendary path with my trusty sticks, through forests and across fields and through villages and cities, scaling immense mountains and inching back down them and spending nearly all that time alone in continual meditation had given me such deep release. My heart was filled with gratitude. It had been important and empowering to spend so much of these weeks alone, and it had been sweet to share the ending with such dear new friends. Now, ten years later, we are still in touch, sending love to one another across oceans via Zoom.

But then, it was time to say goodbye.

Leaving the Camino, I flew back to Paris to decompress for a few days before flying home to Grace. As I walked through the city we had once loved together, I thought about what changes this absence might bring to both our lives. Those last few days I seemed to float through Paris, no longer grounded on the Camino, not yet back to what? My former life? A new version? I didn't know what might lie ahead. I'd been gone for six weeks. But I was changed for the better. I knew I was changed for good.

What a thrill when I found Grace waiting at the gate! Instantly, we were both elated to be back together, although I was the more vocal about it, whooping with joy at the sight of her dear face.

My first night home, she asked me to sleep in her room. She told me that she had been really worried about me, especially during one three-day span when I had no internet access, and she had no idea why she didn't hear from me. I couldn't even get a phone call through, though I had an international phone. Her resentment about taking care of all the household bills herself seemed to have been put aside.

"Ok, you can go back to your own room, now!" she said, after three months had passed. I guess she felt certain then that I was back to stay, that I was home.

On the 20th anniversary of that day when I first heard her dear voice ask, "Miss Stevens?" Grace and I were legally married in the office of her favorite professor at the seminary. Her other beloved professors also came to witness and honor us. After our beautiful ceremony, one of them said, "I have officiated at many weddings; I have attended many weddings, and I think of my own wedding. This wedding today is more meaningful to me than any of those, including my own."

Recently we were talking about how much the Camino changed our relationship, and I asked her why she thought that it had.

"You had to find out who you are. And I had to miss you," said Grace.

Book Four: Comeback

Thirty
Figuring it Out: Breakthrough! 2022

Several months into writing this book, I came across some notes from twenty years ago, when Grace and I were studying with our spiritual teacher who became our dear friend, the late Debbie Ford. I'd written about the first time I attended her signature Shadow Process.

It was a powerfully emotional weekend, where we were encouraged to get in touch with our Shadows, those limiting unconscious beliefs that control our thoughts, words, and behaviors and that consequently control what we feel we deserve to create in our lives. We were helped to better understand ourselves and uncover the information we'd been seeking; knowledge that, for all my years of therapy, I hadn't yet discovered.

In these notes I had written that during a guided visualization process that weekend, an inner Shadow named Angry Anna kept kicking my imaginary meditation seat over and over, trying to get my attention and saying *"your continued collapsing into tears instead of getting angry keeps you from standing in your power."*

Seeing these words now shocked me. How could I have let myself forget such a breakthrough understanding of myself, when I'd been so desperately looking for answers? I felt sick thinking how I had continued to do just that, collapsing into tears in the face of Jenny's anger, all these years.

.

Six years ago, I was reclining in a lounge chair, recovering from shoulder surgery. Grace and I were watching television one evening and the program brought back my longing to travel to Europe again, even though by then Grace was already in her early 70s and I was nearing 80.

"I hope we can make one more trip to Paris, or to Venice before we die," I said.

But Grace snapped, "We can't afford that!"

When I asked her why she was so angry, she said "I've got … responsibilities!" Even though she clammed up, I kept after her.

"What responsibilities?" What was it that I didn't know? What was such a secret?

And then it all came out. Now in her mid-fifties, Jenny had

been cadging money from Grace, telling her that she needed $2500 for her rent, or she would be out on the street, sleeping in her car.

"And don't tell my mother!" Jenny warned. Grace had sent her a $2,500 check a month earlier... but now Jenny had called her again, wanting another $2,500, using the same threats. This time Grace told her she couldn't afford to keep doing this but offered her a few ideas about finding less expensive housing, telling Jenny she was a smart woman, and Grace knew she'd be able to figure it out. Then she hung up.

I exploded! Furious that Jenny had been manipulating Grace. And in that instant, I finally felt the fullness of my anger over her attitude toward me all these years, instead of feeling only my sorrow.

Grace went off to bed, ending the discussion. I stayed in my chair. My anger was so much bigger than my fear of Jenny's rage. It gave me my power at last.

I turned out the light and called out to Jenny, into the darkness: *It's over. We're done. I will not see you again in this lifetime or any other.*

I saw the game that had been there all along. Refusing to let me really know her, and never telling me what the matter was, why she was so angry with me; this was how she held the power. It was as though she was content to remain miserable as long as she knew that my not knowing how to fix it and make her happy was making me miserable too. This had been going on for decades.

Now I felt a calm I'd never known before. I released the breath I was holding. Just as in the moments after my mother's passing, I was free. Now, for the first time in my life, I would no longer be feeling abused by anyone.

In the days and months that followed I saw clearly what a beautiful life I have. How peaceful and loving and kind everyone else is, in my life. Grace is a gift from God, and wonderfully supportive of me in all ways, as I am to her. I thought about my close friends, caring, creative, and fun, and full of lovingkindness. I'm thankful for my gifts as an artist, a numerologist, a coach, and most importantly, as a loving partner and kind friend. I see that with my letting go of the ongoing unhappiness with my daughter, what remains for me is a life full of joy and peace, with gratitude for it all.

I never contacted Jenny again.

Two years later, she mailed a $2,500 check to Grace. The day it arrived, she sent me a short email note telling me I was no longer her mother, and we would not be in contact any more in this lifetime. I didn't respond. I was glad that we were agreed:

no more contact. Finally, truly, it was over for us both. And for the first time ever, without a visit or a phone call full of attack and defense.

I released the person I once loved most in the world, knowing now that neither of us should have had to remain in this relationship that hurt and never healed.

Thirty-One
Big as the Whole Wide World:
Michael – 2021

There are many ways a mother can lose a longed-for child:

- Miscarriage
- Stillbirth
- Fatal Illness
- Runaway
- Suicide
- Drug overdose
- Kidnapping or murder

My loss was none of these.
It was not something I could talk about until now.
My loss was karmic.
In the history of my heartbreaking relationships, I have had

to learn to forgive myself for not knowing how to fix them. Of them all, this is the one that was the most sacred to me - with the child that I had longed for since I was a child myself.

I thought this one would never end. I could not even have imagined it when Jenny was little, and we loved each other so much.

How much?

"Big as the Whole Wide World," she would exclaim, holding her arms open as wide as she could. And I believed her.

"Big as the Whole Wide World," I promised.

There were all the happy times when she was little, and we were riding in the car, laughing and singing our favorite Broadway song from the musical *Gypsy*, about how we'll always be together, no matter what.

Tucking her into bed one night when she was four years old, she sang me a song, instead of waiting for me to sing her a lullaby.

"A girl's best friend is her Mother..." it began.

My eyes filled with tears. "Thank you for your beautiful song, Honey...Sleep tight...Sweet Dreams!" I said, closing her door. I raced to write down all her words I could remember.

In kindergarten she wrote on a pretty note paper, framed by glued-on red plastic popsicle sticks... "*Dear Mother, I love you so much that I can not stant it.*"

Another time she handed me this note..."*Dear Mother, I love you very much. I hope you will exept my apolage. Because I love you very much. I think you are the best mommy in the world. And that is because you take such good care of me. Even when you are mad at me because I have don something rong. I still love you as much as I always do. But I just love you so much I cood scwees you until you are out of breth."*

I found some Mother's Day cards I'd saved from her 20s and 30s. In one of them she wrote...

"This little card sat by itself and looked the least like vous of all, but it called your name because you're my best friend! Remember? "A girl's best friend is her Mom..." It's so true. And I count myself incredibly lucky and grateful to have you as my own. Thank you for giving me life." She enclosed a calendar page that said *"I chose my mother because she was exactly who I needed to enable me to learn and grow."* Jenny added, *"And be the best!"*

Sentiments like these were balm to my heart, but were then followed by years of upsetting encounters during visits filled with inexplicably rude behavior, insults and arguments. Then followed by more endearing cards and apologies. And then more... you see the pattern. Endless.

Recently I saw this on Instagram: "Abuse can't succeed without occasional acts of kindness." Ahh. So.

Then on my 60th Birthday, which fell during the Christmas holidays, Grace and I took her 84-year-old mother to Las Vegas for the weekend, because she wanted to see Celine Dion perform. We invited Jenny to come from Denver and join us there, and she arrived in a great mood, bringing along her friend, Elaine.

When everyone gathered at my birthday dinner that evening, Jenny handed me a gold-framed poem she had written, typed on a paper that was printed with a lovely Mary Cassatt painting of a mother embracing a baby whose sweet head was leaning on Mother's shoulder.

I was astounded. She wrote about always feeling cradled, loved, and nurtured by me. She thanked me for my love that gave her hope, that guided and allowed her to become herself. She even thanked me for my style and my intellect, for sharing my excitement for adventures, and for always being optimistic. She went on to thank me for stretching myself, reaching for balance and growth. She thanked me for my desire to love and be loved. She thanked me for retelling the stores of our lives together, over and over.

She thanked me for letting her go to find herself, and she was grateful I'd given her therapy, instead of college. She even thanked me for letting her know I was sorry that I didn't do everything right in raising her; saying that nobody does. She closed by telling me, once again, that she has always felt this way; cradled, loved, and nurtured by me.

I broke into sobs. This loving acknowledgment, written with such eloquence. I had never dared hope to receive such a gift from my darling difficult daughter.

But then again, the pattern of more painful years followed. *Abuse can't succeed without occasional acts of kindness.*

So, what happened? What could have torn this love away from us both? Was it me? Was I crazy? What had I done? What did I miss? Was it the drugs? Were they the problem? Or the refuge from the problem? Was it the anxiety she finally admitted to having had all her life, that I had never suspected because she kept so privately to herself? Jenny had never confided her feelings, her thoughts, her dreams, or her fears to me from the time she could talk.

Was it a thread of mental illness in our family making its way down to her? There was evidence of that from my grandmother's mumbling, unsmiling, obvious inability to cope, my mother's nervous breakdown when I was a child, and her two faces: one for the public and another for me. And then there were my own suicidal tendencies (before Jenny was born) and my melancholia. How I easily give way to tears, whether I'm happy, sad, frightened or thrilled.

Was I too wrapped up in my work? With my romances? My friends? My dreams for myself?

Well, she had told me I would never know her. And she made sure of it, sharing nothing of her feelings and thoughts, expressing only her anger.

Two years ago, my friend Katie told me of an extraordinary Spirit Guide reading she had experienced with Michael Francis Lott, who is a clairvoyant. I quickly contacted him to ask if he could help me understand Jenny.

I had recently read two books by Robert Schulz, *Your Soul's Gift* and *Your Soul's Plan*. They both explain a concept called pre-birth planning sessions, where a soul meets with a council of Guides prior to birth to plan their upcoming life on Earth. The idea is for us to create a plan for further growth and development that will turn out to be gifts in our life. Other souls are also present at the meeting to decide if they will choose to play their parts in our story.

Michael was familiar with the books and how they explain that there is a reason, a meaning, for the events in our lives that on the surface might seem obscure.

When I asked him about Jenny, giving him only her first name... he listened to my Guides for several minutes and then told me that she had turned away from her Light, and had a highly addictive personality, which I confirmed. I told him how I had always longed to be a mother, and how happy I was when Jenny was born. I talked about how much we had loved each other in those early years, and how heartsick I'd felt for decades. I shared that she had first become angry suddenly at age 5 when she remembered the time when *she* was the Mother, and *I* was the Little Girl. And how much better she liked it that way.

Michael told me that my Guides explained that my daughter and I had been together, helping each other in our growth during other lifetimes, but that we had also often *pinged* guilt back and forth. He said that she had chosen me in this lifetime, because she knew that this time, I could end our relationship now and going forward into future lifetimes.

He went on to talk at length, saying that my Spirit Guides were very excited about a book I was going to be writing. He asked me if I was aware of the book yet, and I said that I did plan to write about my life for a few of my close friends who are much younger. I wanted to share more details about my adventures that have intrigued them, but I felt it was even more important to let them know how I had made it through all the hurts and betrayals and wrong choices in my life. I especially wanted to share with them how I have managed to heal from the wound of losing my only child, finally finding peace and gratitude for my life.

Ever since that first session, Michael has continued to encourage me to write this book. He told me that the Chinese man, the one I first saw in silhouette in my room when I was a baby, was one of my oldest Guides. All my Guides want me to shine my light on this endlessly discouraging situation between parents and adult children. They said that most of them are suffering privately, not wanting even their close friends to know how much they're hurting and how they despair of ever finding healing.

He told me this book will benefit many people, more than I will ever know, because those who feel encouraged to heal themselves from a painful or abusive relationship will tell and inspire others.

Then he added, "The Light that liberates the Light in others, is what lives forever." He said that on another level Jenny knew I needed to live so that I could do this work of freeing her, and writing this book, which is why she has saved my life so many times.

Thirty-Two
HELPING OUT: May others find their healing – 2023

This past year I have been studying with Debra Poneman in her spiritual course "Yes to Success." Experiencing her energy has brought me a huge awareness. Watching her on our Zoom calls each week, I can see Debra's eyes shining with loving kindness for everyone. Both her enthusiasm and her patience seem boundless. Since she had shared her recent birthday with us, I quickly figured that she had a Numerology Life Path #6. I watch how powerfully she is embodying the strength and beauty of this number which brings harmony, counseling, comfort, and care, most especially to marriage and family. But Debra also shares it with the whole world.

What a gift she is for me, as I experience how she brings forward the beauty and compassion of the 6 energies. I see how the lack of the number 6 in my own chart has shown up in my life. And now that I see and feel what is present in her expression, I know what I have been missing and what I am to be learning. It is my Karmic lesson, and a major focus for me in this lifetime.

I wanted to share my thoughts on this with Debra, so I sent her this email...

"Debra...before, I had thought of the lack of Number 6 in my chart as referring only to my marriages and divorces, but now I see it is also to repair myself as a mother. I'd come to feel for so long that I just had to endure the heartbreak around the unhappy relationship with my only child; forever mourning the loss of what I had hoped and truly believed would be my dearest and most fulfilling role.

"But as I finally admitted that I was unable to create that for Jenny and for myself, I came to believe that the even larger lesson is the healing step I've taken in my late 70s...to release myself from our endlessly (mutually) painful relationship. And in the wake of this choice, I found that instead of continuing to torture myself, mourning what is lost, I focused on what remains in my life. There is so much love here and such joy to be embraced. And I found, miraculously, the peace that was waiting for me when I was finally able to let go of the longing for that relationship to change. It was never going to.

"I've wanted to share my story, hoping it will help other parents *and* grown adult children find hope that it is not only okay, but healing, to release yourself from any relationship that seems incapable of functioning in a kind, helpful and loving way.

"For those who struggle with this or similar situations and the anguish that goes with them, I know the guilt and shame they may feel around even the thought of releasing these family bonds. But continuing to tolerate the pain only robs both persons of their chance to become healed and whole, and able to create a better and happier life for themselves.

"Why should we all keep punishing ourselves for failing to find peace with a person who is unkind, intolerant, or in any way unloving toward us even, no, *especially* when it's our own parent or our own adult child?

"I believe that no one deserves to suffer continued heartbreak, to keep enduring such hurtful encounters. Yet to simply disappear and silently become estranged without deep inner reflection may not lead to finding peace either.

"I had to find a third way. What if blessing and releasing them is an even kinder and better gift to give the other, so both may find peace in moving on?

"What I needed, to bring my grief to a closure, was to find a new regard for Jenny and for myself; freeing us both to find our own healing. It was up to me to forgive her and to forgive myself for our human inability to create a relationship with each other that felt loving, supportive, and whole.

"At last, I was able to let her go, wishing the best for her, and determined to create the best for myself, the only one I can ever heal."

Debra answered immediately. "You must publish this! It will help so many!"

In the not-so-distant past, most women stayed married even if they were suffering abuse of any type - emotional, physical, mental, sexual - either for the sake of the children, for religious reasons, or especially because of financial need. Now, however, I believe that most people would advise and support every person, woman or man, who is in an abusive relationship or marriage to find a way to leave, telling their friend that no one should have to suffer.

But breaking the bond between parents and children is still a taboo.

I lived for decades with that ongoing guilt and shame and terrible sadness, being unable to find a way to raise a confident, kind, and caring child. For most of those years I wouldn't speak of our mutual misery even to my closest friends. From what I could see, they and their children seemed to have healthy, cheerful relationships. I was ashamed to admit the truth, that I had failed.

As an eldercare attorney, Grace has told me that in her fifty years of elder-care legal work, she continually sees emotional, and so often financial, abuse by adult children toward their elderly parents (usually mothers) continually. It is epidemic in society. Michael, too, has confirmed how much suffering from emotional abuse he sees in the lives of his clients who are mothers.

I've read reports that many thousands of people, parents and adult children alike, struggle with this same dynamic and are living with the anguish of it, unable to find healing, enduring years of private grief. As I had, they're feeling dread around the thought of letting go of their relationship, of estrangement. Yet both parties in the relationship continue to suffer.

I hope the story of my healing, of finding a third way of resolution, will inspire those who are still hurting– parents and adult children alike – to find peace and forgiveness, most especially for themselves.

For two years, my Guides have continued to cheer me on to write this book. They have told me that writing it has been an assignment that my soul is willing to take on. Along with the support of Grace and my close friends, my Guides have sent me message after message to buoy me up and give me the courage to speak aloud.

Here are excerpts from a few of their messages about this book:

"Write to that mother whose heart is broken. Write to that Adult child who is troubled by a destructive parent. This is about all adult relationships that are hurtful, bringing them to an end, so both can live with peace and comfort. No one deserves to keep suffering. A new day awaits. Lift them up. People are not always bad or wrong, just different. Sometimes you simply cannot reach someone else. Everyone deserves to be free to find love, joy and especially the peace of self-forgiveness."

Another time:

"Give them hope. Bring them peace. Show them love. That is all you need to do. That is why you are here."

And this:

"Write the truth because it will free others from the bondage you suffered. That permission, to deserve a happy life, no matter what, is what is needed and is what your assignment is. You have accomplished this, now go help others. That is all you need to do."

This too:

"It's love! It's all love! It's all about love! Everything is about longing to find love, joy at finding love, fear of losing love, anger at losing love, sorrow at losing love, frantic to find more love, desperate to be loved, longing to give love, gratitude for loving and being loved Again!"

This newfound peace has finally given me what I needed that I didn't have before. Now my hard-earned guideposts can carry me the rest of the way.

I've learned so much about who I am. Through the years I've found deep wisdom and guidance from God, The Divine, All That Is, and through Spiritual Teachers, Numerology, Meditation, Astrology, Therapists, Counselors, and Coaches. I've learned to know my heart, to connect to my spiritual center, to discover my life's purpose, to understand and to identify what qualities of character are most important to me in my relationships with others. Kindness has always been my

Number One. *Thank you, Mrs. Figel, for showing me kindness in second grade and giving me that gift.*

I've learned to be aware of how I'm showing up in life, and how I feel in relationships. Am I still a people-pleaser? Am I allowing myself to be manipulated? Or am I standing in my power?

I've learned to trust my intuition, to be aware of the discomfort that red flags announce. How do I feel in someone's presence? How do I react or respond? How do I feel when I've left their presence? Relieved? Or at ease and looking forward to seeing them again?

I've learned to act from my inner listening in my own best interest. And at last, after all those hard lessons, I've learned to make balanced, realistic choices and decisions.

Most important, I've learned to love myself, knowing that this must be my first loving relationship, because without it, I will be unable to have healthy loving relationships with others.

What I could not repair in my life with Jenny, I've learned to heal in my heart. When I tried to cling to my memories of the past, hoping to recapture the love we had lost, I continually re-created my own suffering. But when I was finally able to let go of what had hurt me, I created space for new and wonderful possibilities.

My heart is so much bigger than the broken places. It holds so much love- for my partner, Grace, for my dear friends, my colleagues, my clients. My life holds so much more than my pain. How can I dwell in that - when there is still so much more love to give, so much more laughter to share while I'm here, so much more awareness to awaken in others' hearts?

Thirty-Three
January 2023

All of that was written over a year ago.

Months later, in the winter, I received a package in the mail. I didn't recognize the handwriting on the label, and there was no return address. I opened it to find three gold necklaces I'd given to Jenny: one when she was a child, one when she was a teenager, and one that was a gift for her high school graduation They were tangled in knots the way tiny gold chains can become when they're left untended for a while.

After the shock of seeing returned to me what I had so long ago given Jenny from my heart, I sat down at the breakfast table with a fine needle and worked for two hours until I untangled each tiny chain. Then I broke them all. It seemed like the appropriate completion of our karma together, breaking the chains that seemed to have bound us for lifetimes. This arrived the day before her 60th birthday. According to her Numerology chart, she was finishing an entire 9-year cycle, and that was the last day of a 9 personal year of endings and completions. She would begin a new 9-year cycle on her birthday, with a 1 personal year of new beginnings. I could see that she was getting herself ready to mark the beginning of a new life, one that I would never be a part of. I knew she knew the significance of it all. She knew I would understand it too.

I had just turned 84 a month earlier, entering a 5 personal year:one of sudden, unexpected events, and change. 84 and 60: those last ages that I had imagined us sharing while I was daydreaming about our lives together on the day she was born.

I set the chains aside, and waited for Spring to arrive when the earth would be soft again. When it was time, my sweet friend Sreemayi, who is a wonderful gardener, came to our home to help me plant the seeds for a new garden. Together we buried the broken golden chains deep in the flower bed, saying our prayers, with a blessing for Jenny and for me.

Epilogue
January 2024

That would have been the end of my story. But then this happened.

I had an appointment with a nurse/practitioner for a checkup. Although I wasn't concerned that anything was wrong, I was on edge about seeing this woman again because she had injured me slightly, but painfully, during a previous visit for a gynecological exam. In addition, she'd seemed unconcerned, even a little rude.

There was no one else in the waiting room, and the air-conditioning was icy. As I waited, feeling uncharacteristically nervous, suddenly I flashed on a time when I had been at a doctor's office with my mother near the end of her life. She had asked me to come to Michigan to go to this appointment with her, and I knew she was frightened. It wasn't like her to ask for my company.

Here in this waiting room, I had the strangest feeling. For the tiniest instant, I felt like I *was* my mother, feeling the fear she had felt that day, so many years ago. Silently in my heart, I burst into tears, calling out to her now: *Oh, Mommy! You never had anyone to tell your secrets to! You kept it all inside! I am sorry you suffered so silently all your life!*

When the exam was over and I got back inside my car, I cried aloud, telling my mother over and over again that now, at last, I understood her pain. Even though I didn't know the reasons; how sorry I felt that she had never found relief. Now I realized what a valiant effort she had made to be gracious to friends and strangers, even though the mask dropped off at home with me. I told her what an incredible job she had done at keeping the household running, making it beautiful, paying the bills, and feeding us delicious meals all those years. I thanked her again and again for all she had done to give me a wonderful education, especially in the arts, and how glad I am that she had made sure I was kept healthy.

With deep remorse, I apologized for dropping out of the university my parents had paid for, when they'd been so proud of me for the beautiful artwork I was creating in my classes. I thanked her for taking me back into their home when I left Jack and came back to the States pregnant with Jenny, whom she loved so much. How sorry I was that I had taken Jenny away to New York, remembering that my mother didn't try to spoil my excitement about taking on that adventure by making me wrong for trying, even as it must have hurt her awfully to see Jenny go.

After that conversation in the car, I began to listen for my mother's voice. I felt that she was telling me that she had been waiting 30 years to reach me, ever since she'd passed away, hoping for my forgiveness for the switchings and the criticism. Since that day a few months ago, I have continued to feel her warmly nearby.

Soon I stumbled across recipes online for two of my favorite dishes she had cooked for me in my childhood, and recreating them now made me feel her presence, even her guidance, in the kitchen. I have even begun to enjoy cooking, which had never appealed to me until now.

The following month I "accidentally" came across two books online: *Difficult Mothers, Adult Daughters* and *You Are Not Your Mother* both written by Karen C.L. Anderson, a life coach who is about my daughter's age. I devoured them and immediately I could see our relationship, our lives together, especially myself in my mothering role, through Jenny's eyes.

These books were an extraordinary awakening. I wish I could summarize all I saw revealed in them. Their information and viewpoints were new to me, even after all my years of searching.

If this is your story, please get them. Whether you're the Mother *or* the Adult Daughter, they will speak deeply to you.

Reading them brought a profound shift, emotionally and

mentally. My mind's previous version of what our lives had been like together was no longer my truth.

I now saw that drugs could have been Jenny's refuge from her anxiety, and that her refusal to let me know her might have been her protection, and her claim to have her own self, a defense against what I learned was my codependency. I saw that what had seemed like adventures to me, must have been tearing her from whatever roots had been tentatively forming in her young life.

One of the many beautifully healing statements that the author, Karen C.L. Anderson, makes is this: *Emotional separation is the solution and the medicine, not the thing that needs to be fixed or healed. You don't need to "make peace" with it, because it is peace.*

For the first time in years, I went to an app on my phone where I knew Jenny's business was listed. I hoped there would be some evidence that she was still alive, and even thriving. There was a timeline of recent projects, including a mention that she had recently edited a book by a former therapist of ours in Dallas. Jenny had first been a client of hers over thirty years ago, and I had been her client twenty years ago.

This therapist, whom I'll call Sally, had been a warm, compassionate woman of great integrity and Solomon-like wisdom. I was filled with such respect and admiration for her. Once, when Jenny was in her early 30s, we had a joint session with Sally, both of us describing our own difficulties in our relationship. At the close of the session, Sally suggested that we take a 6-month break from communicating, and just enjoy our own lives, without fighting these battles.

Now, suddenly finding the news of their recent close connection, and filled with my new awareness of what our relationship might have been like for Jenny, I had hope that I would be able to make an amends to her. And in my heart, I felt Sally would be willing to do this for both of us.

Making amends is such a vital part of the 12-Step Programs that had meant so much to me 35 years ago, helping me to quit smoking. And Jenny had once done a 12-Step program for her drug addiction, so I knew amends would be familiar to her.

I found Sally's contact information and called her, leaving a voicemail, asking her for an appointment. She texted me back quickly, saying how nice it was to hear from me and offering me a session the next afternoon.

As soon as I walked in the door and saw her standing there, twenty years evaporated. I was so grateful to see her, to feel her wise and comforting energy, always offering that feeling that all is well, or will be, shortly, if you take good care of yourself.

I was nervous and excited with all that was happening, from

first discovering Sally's recent connection with Jenny to this moment in her loving presence. Immediately I asked her if Jenny was alive, and well.

"Oh, yes! She's moved to another part of California and she's happy. Her business is very successful, with big clients, and she has a dog!" Sally reported.

A dog? We'd always been cat people. And then I knew she had moved on; I could feel it. She *has* created a new life. How wonderful! She's happy and successful. It brought me joy, knowing this, realizing I felt as if I were just hearing good news of someone I'd once known.

I leaned into the pillows on the couch, while Sally was in a swivel chair pulled up near me. I opened the two books that had changed everything about how I had seen myself in my role as a mother all these decades. And I began telling her how they opened me up to seeing Jenny's pain and consequent anger in a new light.

I showed her page after page full of blue and orange circles and exclamation marks I'd made to help me remember the words that had blasted my old ideas away. Sally listened intently while I sobbed through reading so many of the words that had awakened me.

Then I poured out the pain of my childhood with my mother's switchings and endless criticism. I spoke with wonder about my astonishing experience in the doctor's office waiting room, when I began seeing and feeling my mother's pain for the first time, crying out to her how sorry I was that she'd carried it all inside.

"I want to make amends to Jenny," I said. "But I don't want to contact her. I'm not asking for her forgiveness. In 12-Step parlance, I want to sweep my side of the street. I'm so glad to know that she's creating a wonderful life for herself, and I don't want to interrupt it. I feel we are both better apart. Would you be willing to be a conduit for this?"

"Of course," Sally responded. "I don't know when or how I will give her your amends, whether I'll send it in an email or read it to her. I'll ask my Angels and Guides to help me feel for when and how. I don't know for sure that she will want to read it, but I do feel certain that she'll be very interested in hearing how this all came about."

Sally was feeling emotional too, and we agreed that this was, indeed, "a God deal."

We made an appointment for the following week when I would return with my amends letter.

Here is my letter, which I read aloud to Sally, swallowing my tears as I read.

Dear Jenny,

I am writing to you to make amends to you for all that has hurt you, in whatever way I have done – or failed to do – to give you the guidance you needed and deserved when I was your mother. I am deeply sorry.

I have felt decades of anguish, feeling that I failed to become the mother you might have wanted, but never received.

This past month I read two books that deepened my understanding of mother/daughter patterns in ways I'd never known before.

After reading them, I wanted to be able to tell you these things and make my amends to you.

First, I want to apologize for taking you to New York when you were only two and a half years old, away from your grandparents who loved you, and away from your Ten Little Indians school where you were so happy. Having to place you in the nursery school in New York that brought you suffering, broke my heart for you, daily. I was devastated that I had done this to you. I am so very sorry.

Because my mother had never shared her thoughts and feelings and dreams with me, I never felt close to her. I was determined not to be like that with you, but I see now how I went overboard and inappropriately shared my thoughts and feelings with you from the time you were much too young. I'm horrified to realize what an enormous burden it must have been for you. Now I understand why some of our friends would say during your teen years that it seemed like you were the mother and I was the little girl. (How ironic.)

Another enormous regret is that I had no real understanding of child development. What I see now is that even though teenage rebellion is necessary, it doesn't necessarily mean that the teenager doesn't love the parent. I am so sorry that I took your rebellion so personally. I was afraid that your anger meant that I was losing your love, and I failed to be a strong parent for you.

Another most important regret is that I never understood

about drugs. They terrified me. I am so sorry that I didn't know how to deal with that issue with you, and that it distanced us further.

I was not a strong person in my relationships with men, and I see how I failed to give you a healthy example and the guidance you deserved. I am so sorry that I didn't provide you with a stable home life by marrying a man who could have been a good and strong father for you.

I want to apologize for being a poor example on handling money, always living beyond my means, and then always needing to be rescued. I am so very sorry.

I have written a book about my life, my adventures, my lessons. It includes our time together, which is a very important part. (I have not used your name.)

In it, I am talking to both parents and adult children about the healing that is possible with letting go of a painful relationship when there is such ongoing emotional turmoil that it seems unlikely ever to heal. In such a case, I feel that the mutually compassionate decision is to say goodbye, to let the wounds heal, and to embrace the peace.

It is grace to have this opportunity to give you my amends, with Sally's help, who feels such compassion for us both.

I wish you everything good in your life. And I hope this amends can bring you some peace. May you be well.

This is given to you with Love and Compassion for us both.

For as long as I can remember, I have been terrified of driving on highways. I feared I would be in a horrible, even fatal accident, as the punishment that was waiting for me for, what? I had no idea. With my new understanding from these books, I see it's been because of the shame and guilt I have been carrying all my life, first as a daughter and then, as a mother.

But that day, driving home on the highway after speaking aloud my amends for Jenny in that soul-comforting hour with Sally, that fear left me. I knew then that I deserve to live in peace, without fear.

I felt I had completed my work as a mother in this lifetime. Even if Jenny never responds.

The next morning, I sent a thank you email to Sally:

Thank you for listening with your heart open to me, even with your love for Jenny. I thought I felt your pain for what she had suffered as my daughter, as you listened to me recite my sorrowful apologies for what I had done or failed to do as her mother.

Your compassion for me, even so, means so much. Thank you. I'm forever grateful to you, and to God – and to Karen C.L. Anderson, the author of these books that began this healing, this incredible gift.

A few hours later, this response from Sally:

. . .

My dear Sherle,

Thank you for sharing these thoughts and feelings with me. You are a wonderful communicator. You are a wonderful Soul as is Jenny. You both have done many things right – please remember that, as you are only human, and we are all doing the best we can at any point in time with the awareness, understanding and the knowledge that we have at that time.

You clearly have grown as has Jenny, because of one another, even if that might not make sense to you.

That is why relationships are sacred, because they are the mirrors through which we can see ourselves and evolve if we choose to. You have chosen to. My joy for you is great now that you feel free and at peace.

I have asked my Guides and my Angels to assist me in being the messenger of love and understanding to Jenny and truly believe only good will come from it. When the time is right, I will share your letter and your intent.

Now just relax and enjoy your life knowing you are brave and loving and a true thriver after surviving some unloving actions from your misguided mother.

You deserve all good. Not some, not a little bit, but all good!

Namaste, Sally

What a kind benediction.

Three days later, Jenny wrote an email to me:

. . .

Subject Line: ...*Blessings All Around...*

Hi Sherle –

I received your letter and am glad to hear that you're moving on, in peace. As always, I wish you all the best.

Love, Namaste,

Jenny

And it is done. We are complete. We are both blessed. We are Free.

☙

I'm so grateful for my life. Even though I was once afraid I couldn't bear it, I have. Even though I thought the heartbreaks would kill me, I have grown from them.

A few weeks ago, I turned 85. Now, as I'm finishing up my story, it's nearly Jenny's 61st Birthday. In 26 hours from now, it will be the time of her birth – and it will mark the completion of our time together that I had first imagined on the day she was born...*and when she's 60 I'll be 84*... How fascinating that I've always remembered these ages, never dreaming of their significance.

☙

This morning in my meditation, when I went to my heart center, I was surprised to see that everyone I had ever loved was still there. No matter what had happened to end each relationship, the original love I'd felt had never left me. What a gift of grace to know this. And to feel it filling my heart.

In the center and beaming brightly, was Jenny, my dear girl. There in the quiet, I felt the tears. But now no longer from pain. This time I felt the joy of knowing that despite anything later broken, love doesn't die. It's big as the whole wide world.

Afterword
Running Out of Time: And wanting to leave a few more notes for you

Writing this book has healed me of my movie fantasies. I've awakened to the dream of life, which is real and far more precious than I could have imagined.

Although I'm sure I will always be a weenie when it comes to physical pain, I'm no longer afraid of the transition of dying, of letting go of this life and returning to the Divine Source I have felt near me always, ever since I first knew I could return there to find a new Mommy and Daddy.

Experiencing this protracted life review, rereading old letters from so long ago, finding information online about those I've loved and lost; this has been such a gift. The tears, the frustrations, the lagging behind my own self-structured deadline, the words that would write themselves in my head even while having dinner in a restaurant; this writing has become a living organism of its own that I never imagined.

Afterword

I highly recommend the process. I encourage you to do your own life review, at whatever age you are willing to reach for it. Yes, it will bring tears, regrets, maybe even some embarrassment. I know it has been all of that for me. But there is so much more. It also holds joy, gratitude and a new, deeper understanding and appreciation for the people who have loved you, who have taught you, who have inspired you, and who otherwise got your attention in some way that gave you another leg up on your journey.

Certainly, most importantly, writing your story is an opportunity to forgive those who've hurt you, and even better, the chance for you to ask in your heart (at least) for forgiveness from others, and beyond that, to find forgiveness for yourself.

Here's the incredible reward for your willingness and courage in looking back. You will find a kind of awe at the astounding person you've become. Look at all you've dared: the people you dared to love, the work you dared to take on, the places you've dared to go, in the world, and within yourself.

Look at the photos that have recorded your childhood. Pause and see what you remember about the day a particular photo was taken. What was happening? Who was there with you? What were you feeling? Did you make some sort of decision about yourself - or someone else because of something that happened that day?

Look at your high school pictures and notice how you began to grow from a child into a young adult. As you see the photos of your friends, recall some of the days you spent with them. What did you do together? Where did you go when you could finally drive a car?

What was it like to fall in love? Or be rejected? Who did you say goodbye to? When did you know what you most wanted to do with your life? Which dreams have you tried to make come true? And which ones have you kept hidden in your heart - afraid to claim?

I have a cartoon pinned on my studio wall from *The New Yorker* magazine. It shows an open-bed truck overflowing with something puffy in it that it's delivering to a big, tall building. All the windows in the building are full to overflowing with more of that same puffy stuff . The caption says: "The Abandoned Dreams Depot." I keep it there to remind myself to live as many of my dreams as I can while I'm still here.

Which relationships have worked out and which have not? Where are those people now? What experiences have been worth the effort, the uphill fight? Which failures led eventually to higher ground?

What goals have inspired you to reach higher? Hopefully there are several. What has given you faith in the goodness of life? What are you most proud of? What gives you hope?

This is a profound opportunity to find love in your heart for the incredible ride this life has been so far. Your review can be a time rich with thanksgiving, for others and for yourself. Let it be a celebration of this truly astonishing experience.

Afterword

It continues to amaze me that the body I'm in now is the same body I arrived here in. I didn't shed my baby body the way a snake sheds it's skin. These legs that just walked me down the hall are the same legs that took my first steps. My dyed-red hair, which has decided to curl in my old age, is growing from the same head that my youthful thick straight black hair emerged from. Isn't this journey a miracle?

But that's not who I am, this body. I am still the baby who found the courage to stay, in spite of heartbreak, for chocolate. I'm still the good little girl who loved her paper dolls and books and feared her mother. There I am, still the high school girl who couldn't wait to leave home, trying to find love and dazzling success in New York. Three times. And there I am, always the newly divorced mother whose dreams of loving a child of her own finally came true, even though the daddy was gone. I am the emotionally exhausted old woman who found the courage to say goodbye to her middle-aged daughter when ultimately, they couldn't find peace together, and I'm the frightened woman who answered the call to the pilgrimage of the Camino and who returned, finally standing in the fullness of her power, to create a new relationship with Grace.

I will always be the dreamer, the lover, the friend.

Holding all of that, I'll still be watching the horizon, longing for one more adventure that I might squeeze in before I'm gone.

Now imagine -What might be waiting for you?

About the Author

Throughout her life, Sherle Stevens has navigated the complex journey of difficult family relationships, unhealthy romantic entanglements, and the emotional turmoil of childhood trauma. Her story is a testament to her strength and her unwavering commitment to living a healed life.

In this deeply personal and transformative memoir, she explores the taboo of estrangement, bringing insight for finding healing to those who suffer in silence, in secrecy, and shame. Sharing her own journey of healing and self-discovery, she offers readers insights and strategies for overcoming their own struggles. With compassion and wisdom, she guides us through the process of healing unresolved karmic connections and finding peace.

Today, Sherle continues to paint in her studio, infusing her work with the same passion and intensity that has always made her feel most alive.

She lives just outside Dallas, Texas with her partner, Grace and their family; Lincoln, the Great Pyrenees, Phoenix, the Schnauzer, and Tutti, the cat.

Bigasthewholewideworld.com

SherleStevens.com

SherleStevensStudio.com

Her first book, *The Numerology Playbook*, is also available on Amazon.

Acknowledgments

I am so thankful for the wonderful life I have been given. The love I share with Grace, truly the mate of my soul, continues to delight and sustain me. Always, I have received so much love and shared such joy with my dear friends, most especially Larry Talley, my Cosmic Playmate, Catherine and Matt Milliken, Lea Marlin, Beth Speiser, Tink Davis, Katie Carlone, Thressa Connor, Alexia Georgousis, Marla Sandberg, Sydarta Thorsdottir, and Sharon Midkiff, who recently invited me to return to the beloved lake of my childhood in Michigan. I thank each one of you for sharing your endearing love, your humor and insight, and your beautiful spirit.

My studies with the spiritual teachers and authors who've inspired me over the past fifty years have expanded my conscious awareness and opened my heart even further. Most especially with our dear friend, the late Debbie Ford, and with Ram Dass, Stephen Levine, Jean Houston, Caroline Myss, Andrew Harvey, Debra Poneman, and Sam Bennett. I am so thankful to have discovered the work of Karen C.L.Anderson, whose writings enabled me to open my heart to see the other side of my story, through the eyes of someone else's daughter. And I am immensely grateful to Michael Francis Lott, for sharing the messages from my Guides, who wanted me to write this book.

From that beginning, I have felt guided to find everyone I needed to complete this project. I discovered my extraordinary editor, Anne Stockwell. Her understanding, care and insight when reading my first draft inspired me to write further until I had created a fully realized book. Her cheers when I finished, were everything. When I was ready to design my book's cover, I met Heather Gaughan, graphic designer/web designer, whose cover design and beautiful photograph of her own lily-pads (my favorite flower) were instant perfection. Heather introduced me to Michelle Stimpson, my publisher, a tech genius and creative, too, who has worked with me side-by-side to put this all together. I feel such gratitude for these two women, who are pure gold. I also give thanks to the WOW - Write On Waxahachie - the writers' group in the nearby county seat, where we meet every Wednesday afternoon at the Sims Library. Thank you all for listening to me read my story, chapter by chapter.

Before I wrote this book I was an illustrator and a painter for sixty-five years and a numerologist for the past fifty years. Helping my clients embrace the beauty and strength of their soul's blueprint in my numerology readings continues to bring me great joy. My lifelong work as an artist is still a source of wonder. *As in I wonder when I'm going to get back to painting? Well,* not until this book is in your hands.

Resources

Katie Carlone, Master Coach & Life Strategist; Spiritual Advisor, Astrologer https://katiecarlone.com

Michael Francis Lott, Clairvoyant, Intuitive https://theblossomingself.com michaelfrancislott@gmail.com

Debra Poneman, Author & Spiritual Teacher, Founder of Yes To Success & Ageless Seminars https://YesToSuccess.com

Sam Bennett, Author: Get It Done, Start Right Where You Are, and The 15-Minute Method 2024. https://therealsambennett.com and on LinkedIn

Anne Stockwell, Editor Extraordinaire, Find her on LinkedIn

RESOURCES

Karen C.L. Anderson, Master-certified Life Coach and author of several books including: *You Are Not Your Mother: Releasing Generational Trauma and Shame* and *Difficult Mothers, Adult Daughters: A Guide for Separation, Liberation, and Inspiration.* She is also the host of the Dear Adult Daughter Podcast and founder of Shame School

Michelle Stimpson, Publisher
https://www.MichelleStimpson.com

Heather Gaughan, Cover Designer, Photographer and Website Designer
https://www.heathergaughan.com/

Sherle Stevens, *The Numerology Playbook*, on Amazon

**The first books that gave me answers;
Classics that are still available on Amazon**

Yoga, Youth & Reincarnation by Jess Stearn 1965

Seth Speaks, by Jane Roberts 1972 (loved by Deepak Chopra, Marianne Williamson and Louise Hay)

Be Here Now, by Ram Dass 1971

You Were Born Again To Be Together, by Dick Sutphen revised edition 2021

Resources

You Can Heal Your Life, by Louise Hay 1984

You Can Heal Your Body, by Louise Hay 1984

The Dynamic Laws of Healing, by Catherine Ponder 1966

The Dynamic Laws of Prosperity, by Catherine Ponder 1962

Many Lives, Many Masters, by Brian Weiss 1988

Books that continue to inspire me:

Walking Each Other Home, by Ram Dass 2019

A Year To Live, by Stephen Levine 1998

Your Soul's Plan by Robert Schulz 2009

My own websites:

bigasthewholewideworld.com

SherleStevens.com Numerology consultations

SherleStevensStudio.com Art

www.ingramcontent.com/pod-product-compliance
Lightning Source LLC
Chambersburg PA
CBHW052103280426

43673CB00084B/444/J